"Oh sing to the L<small>ORD</small> *a new song,*
for He has done marvelous things!"

Psalm 98:1

Save Me, O My God!

Psalms of Lament

CONCORDIA PUBLISHING HOUSE · SAINT LOUIS

a new song

Save Me, O My God!
Psalms of Lament

Meet the Authors

Jane L. Fryar enjoys serving God's people by writing and teaching. Her books include two titles focused on Servant Leadership, several LifeLight Bible study courses, the popular Today's Light devotional materials, and various other curriculums and resources for Christian teachers. Jane spends her spare time baking bread, lifting weights, and playing with Marty the Wonder Dog.

Judith Meyer serves as Minister of Discipling at Prince of Peace Lutheran Church, Springfield, Virginia. She and her husband enjoy long walks in downtown Washington DC and traveling to visit their children and grandchildren. She wishes she had more time to devote to writing children's stories.

Jane Wilke is convinced that life is a journey of amazing twists and turns. Along the way she has transitioned from being a teacher to an editor to a creative director to a specialist in communications. She loves traveling with her husband, is a frequent speaker, has a weekly inspirational radio spot, and looks forward to what God might have in mind for her around the next corner.

Carla Fast, wife of Pastor Thomas Fast and mother to Christopher, is fascinated with words. As such, in addition to writing, she enjoys teaching English and literature. She relishes discussing grammar and diagramming English sentences (it can be a lonely world!). The word she loves most, however, is that first loved us—the Word made flesh.

Rose E. Adle lives in Secor, Illinois, with her husband Scott. He is pastor of St. John's Lutheran. Together they enjoy playing games, cooking, and reading. Some of Rosie's other interests include Spanish, tennis, and travel. More recently she's kept busy entertaining visiting family and friends and getting a room ready for their first baby on the way.

Terry Lee Kieschnick, a pastor's wife, says it has been her privilege to serve the Lord with joy, "blooming" personally through professional and spiritual experiences and in ministry partnership with her husband, Jerry, president of The Lutheran Church—Missouri Synod. She enjoys her role as "Mimi" and serving with Jerry throughout the Synod and around the world, speaking and writing, to the glory of God.

Cynda Strong teaches high school English in Springfield, Illinois. She lives outside the city with her husband, Micheal, a retired minister. They have two children, Adam and Rebecca, and two grandchildren, who keep her joyfully busy. Her hobbies include quilting and Elizabethan history. Cynda has published two children's picture books *(Where Do Angels Sleep?* and *Did Noah Take Termites on the Ark?)* and has been published in *Today's Christian Woman.*

*Arise, O L*ORD*!*
Save me, O my God!
For You strike all my
enemies on the cheek;
You break the teeth of
the wicked. Psalm 3:7

Contents

How to Use This Book

A New Song: Save Me, O My God! is designed to help you grow in faith in your Savior, Jesus Christ, and to see how God works in your life as His precious and redeemed daughter. It is not meant to consume large blocks of your time. Rather, this book will help you to weave God's Word into your day. It will also encourage and uplift you in your personal and small-group study of His Word.

A New Song: Save Me, O My God! provides you and your group with six weeks of faith narratives based on selected psalms. Each faith narrative was written by a real woman facing real-life issues—just like you. Each of our authors found help, encouragement, and direction for her life from God's Word and now shares her true story with you in her own words. Following each faith narrative, you will find questions that will encourage your own personal reflection and help bring forth meaningful and fruitful conversation in the comfort and security of your small group.

To derive the greatest benefit from your study, read the psalm in its entirety at the beginning of the week, and review it from time to time. Allow the authors' reflections on God's work in their lives to inspire your own. Write your responses and thoughts in the margins, if you wish. Space is provided on the side of each page under the 🖋 symbol. Answer the daily questions as best fits your unique situation and the time available to you, but consider how your responses can further group discussion. The prayers offered at the end of each narrative will help you to focus on the weekly theme and emphasis as you respond to God for His gifts of grace. Use the prayers as they are written, or make them your own, changing and adding to them as they touch your heart.

Our prayer is that this book will enrich you as you look to our God and Savior—the victor over all our enemies—in your study of His Holy Word.

—The Editor

Suggestions for Small-Group Participants

1. Before you begin, spend some time in prayer, asking God to strengthen your faith through the study of His Word. The Scriptures were written so that we might believe in Jesus Christ and have life in His name (John 20:31).

2. Take some time before the meeting to look over the session, review the psalm, and answer the questions.

3. As a courtesy to others, arrive on time.

4. Be an active participant. The leader will guide the group's discussion, not give a lecture.

5. Avoid dominating the conversation by answering every question or by giving unnecessarily long answers. On the other hand, avoid the temptation to not share at all.

6. Treat anything shared in your group as confidential until you have asked for and received permission to share it outside of the group. Treat information about others outside of your group as confidential until you have asked for and received permission to share it with group members.

7. Some participants may be new to Bible study or new to the Christian faith. Help them feel welcomed and comfortable.

8. Affirm other participants when you can. If someone offers what you perceive to be a "wrong" answer, ask the Holy Spirit to guide her to seek the correct answer from God's Word.

9. Keep in mind that the questions are discussion starters. Don't be afraid to ask additional questions that relate to the topic. Don't get the group off track.

10. If you are comfortable doing so, volunteer now and then to pray at the beginning or end of the session.

Jane L. Fryar

Introduction

Two years and two weeks. That's how long it took 56-year-old Karen Thorndike to sail around the world in her little sailboat, the *Amelia*. Bobbing along the 33,000 miles of her journey, Thorndike encountered hailstorms, bone-numbing cold, searing heat, and attacks of angina. Most of us can scarcely imagine the challenges she describes in her logs, let alone dream what motivated her to attempt the challenge.

The prospect of typhoons and the certainty of sharks

would dissuade most of us from mounting an adventure like Thorndike's. While the dangers would be off-putting enough, the specter of two years in isolation from other human beings would probably loom even larger. Thorndike, you see, sailed solo.

This volume in the A New Song series focuses on psalms that express, among other trials, the pain of extreme loneliness. All begin on a note Karen Thorndike might easily recognize. The psalmists encounter challenges in life that threaten to capsize them, to overwhelm their meager spiritual resources.

Spurred on by their need, they cry out to the Lord. As they do, hope and help seem 33,000 miles (or more!) away. Perhaps God has forgotten them. Perhaps He has forgotten His promises, His commitment to justice and compassion. Fear threatens to drown them, as confusion, pain, and need swamp their hearts.

And yet, far away and detached though they may feel, the psalmists are not alone. God has not abandoned them, nor has He become their enemy. He knows the pain they endure. He hears the insults and accusations Satan hurls. His heart goes out in compassion to His children.

Interestingly, none of the psalmists detail the circumstances that evoked their words of lament. While Bible scholars have teased out some logical possibilities and rabbinic tradition gives a few clues, we do not know for sure when or why any of the psalms in this volume were written. Some have suggested that the Holy Spirit oversaw and even directed this anonymity so you and I can read our own pain, our own life challenges into the texts.

Waves of Distress

Each of the six psalms we will examine in this book comes at us from a slightly different angle. Each will call on us to trim our sails in a slightly different way as we read and apply it. As we do, careful readers will quickly discern similar patterns of concern in each psalm.

Consider, for example, the issue of justice as it recurs in these Psalms of Lament. Why do people who hate God and make life miserable for His people enjoy a life of fair skies, moderate temperatures, and calm seas? Why do they sail along unperturbed, while hailstones rain down on God's own day after day? Why must we shiver in the arctic winds of their lies and gossip, while they never seem to face the consequences of their actions?

Or think about the recurring issues of sin and righteousness (our own!). While we join the psalmists in their rage at the false accusations launched against us by our enemies, we know deep down that we cannot really claim to be innocent. In fact, we know that many of the accusations our enemies hurl at us are true. We have sinned. Standing in guilt up to our necks, how can we insist that our Lord avenge us against our attackers? How can we assert the rightness of our cause when we know full well that we deserve God's just judgment every bit as much as those who hurt us by their sin? How can we pray "Jesus, Savior, pilot me, over life's tempestuous seas" as we sit awash in rebellion against God and disobedience to His will?

As wave after wave of guilt crashes into our boat, despair washes over us. Adrift in a sea of anguish, we echo the lamentations of the psalmists—Spirit-inspired words—to express the thoughts and feelings that torment us.

An Ocean of Hope

With the psalmists, then, we watch the clouds part and the storm die away as the truth dawns anew upon our hearts. The promises of our Savior-God trump every other reality:

- ❋ The Lord is our shield. (Psalm 3:3; 5:12; 7:10)
- ❋ The holy God listens to our prayers, accepts, and answers them! (Psalm 3:4; 4:3; 6:8–9)
- ❋ God "spreads [His] protection over" anyone and everyone who takes refuge in Him. (Psalm 5:11)
- ❋ Through the "abundance of [His] steadfast love" (Psalm 5:7), we—though sinful—may enter our Lord's presence in bold confidence, relying on His continuing love.
- ❋ God gives salvation (Psalm 3:8), righteousness and re-

lief (Psalm 4:1), joy (Psalm 4:7; 5:11), peace (Psalm 4:8), healing (Psalm 6:2), strength and justice (Psalm 10:17) to His people. And He gives these things purely as His gifts to us—no strings attached.

We do not and cannot earn or deserve these blessings, but they are ours because God is gracious to us in Christ's cross. Adrift on the high seas of feelings, tossed about by the winds and waves of our daily circumstances, we may find ourselves bewildered, enraged, hurt, fearful, and needy. But we are never forgotten. Never! We are always loved. *Always!*

No matter how great our guilt or overwhelming our problems, we enter heaven's throne room as Christ's holy people, His redeemed saints. We see in His outstretched hands of welcome the nail scars by which He won our full forgiveness. We can present our case before heaven's High King, already knowing His verdict. We enjoy His favor. He takes our side. He Himself defends us.

When tears fill our eyes, when we choke on our words because of the lump in our throats, when we cannot form a coherent thought or speak a meaningful sentence, the Spirit Himself gives us the words we need. He prays in us and for us, just as He has promised (Romans 8:26–27). So, we say with confidence:

As a mother stills her child,
Thou canst hush the ocean wild;
Boist'rous waves obey Thy will
When Thou say'st to them, "Be still!"
Wondrous Sov'reign of the sea,
Jesus, Savior, pilot me
(LSB 715:2).

Week One

Psalm 3

[1] O LORD, how many are my foes!
Many are rising against me;

[2] many are saying of my soul,
there is no salvation for him in God. *Selah*

[3] But You, O LORD, are a shield about me,
my glory, and the lifter of my head.

[4] I cried aloud to the LORD,
and He answered me from His holy hill. *Selah*

[5] I lay down and slept;
I woke again, for the LORD sustained me.

[6] I will not be afraid of many thousands of people
who have set themselves against me all around.

[7] Arise, O LORD!
Save me, O my God!
For You strike all my enemies on the cheek;
You break the teeth of the wicked.

[8] Salvation belongs to the LORD;
Your blessing be on Your people! *Selah*

Judith Meyer

Psalm 3:1–2

O LORD, how many are my foes!
Many are rising against me; many are saying
of my soul, there is no salvation for him in God. Selah

Christic, the Victor

King David's life was the stuff of soap-operas—murder, betrayal, adultery, and intrigue. How devastating it must have been to be betrayed by his son, Absalom! Among the lessons we can learn from David's life are where to take our problems and whom to call for

help. What strikes me about the first two verses of Psalm 3 is the urgency in David's words. He was not discussing his problem with Bathsheba over morning coffee or complaining to his best friend, Jonathan. With a heavy and fearful heart, David was crying out to the Lord God, confident that He would listen—and act!

In September 2002, my husband and I moved to northern Virginia, just outside the Washington DC Beltway. I had a new call as a lay minister to a congregation much larger and more cosmopolitan than the two suburban Florida congregations I'd served previously. I eagerly anticipated the smorgasbord of cultural events at my doorstep, and I looked forward to the challenges my new position presented. Everything seemed new and exciting!

While my husband and I knew this would be a big change for us, I confess I was not prepared for the culture shock of the Beltway, that famous sixty-four-mile-long interstate that encircles the District of Columbia and a few Maryland and Virginia suburbs. You probably know that the phrase *inside the Beltway* refers less to geography and more to matters of government and politics. For those who work inside the Beltway, knowing the enemy is fairly easy—they probably belong to the other political party. Clearly, what matters is not *what* you know, but *who* you know. The battle lines are clear. Power equals influence, and influence is expressed in terms of the number of handshakes away you are from a congressperson, an agency chief, or the president and whose phone numbers are in your speed dial.

Meeting the members of our new congregation and discovering where they worked fascinated us. My husband came home from his first choir rehearsal and remarked, "I'm the only one in the bass section who didn't graduate from one of the military academies! The guy next to me is a retired four-star!"

We also found ourselves unprepared for the remnants of the shock and pain that lingered among our new friends just twelve months after the 9/11 attack on the Pentagon. Repairs to the damaged building were progressing rapidly, but the emotional wounds of the workers and citizens would take much longer to heal.

One of the first women I met who had worked at the

Judith

Pentagon lost forty friends that awful day. She'd decided to move her family to South Carolina to escape the post-traumatic stress. Shortly before they moved, she shared with me that she could no longer trust anyone. She suspected the new family down the block was part of a terrorist cell. At a security checkpoint at Reagan National Airport, an innocent Sikh man wearing a turban so unnerved her that she almost missed her flight. What frightened her most, she said, was the feeling of helplessness—knowing an enemy is out there but not being able to identify it and not knowing where to turn for help.

During our first weeks in our new home, the Department of Homeland Security threat level remained "elevated." Then, just about the time we unpacked the last box and the oak leaves were showing off their autumn colors, a new, nameless, faceless enemy appeared. The DC snipers terrorized the area for twenty-three days in October 2002, killing ten victims and wounding three more as they went about the normal business of life—mowing the grass, loading groceries, pumping gas, going to school. The anxiety was palpable. Police warned citizens to stay alert and report anything suspicious. The search was on for two men and a white van. For three anxious weeks, I looked differently at every van I encountered, white or otherwise, and scrutinized every car next to me at a traffic signal, wondering, Is that them? When police finally apprehended the killers, the city breathed a huge sigh of relief. The enemy had been identified and dealt with. Life could return to normal.

You and I can laugh in the face of our foes rather than listen to their taunts because we know that Christ is the victor for us. We are eternally connected to Him and to His victory over death and hell through our Baptism.

David, the great king of Israel and a man after God's own heart, was not immune to anxiety and Satan's tactics. David's psalms read like his personal diary, expressing both despair and hope in a testimony to his faith. Some of the devil's attacks upon him were annoyances; others meant life or death. David's faith showed him where to go for help.

When I think of the foes David refers to in the first two vers-

Judith

es of Psalm 3, these words of the hymn "A Mighty Fortress Is Our God" immediately come to mind:

> *The old satanic foe has sworn to work us woe.*
> *With craft and dreadful might he arms himself to fight.*
> *On earth he has no equal.* (LSB 657:1)

We know that Satan works overtime to create chaos in our lives, to disrupt, annoy, aggravate, frustrate, and generally make life difficult. He loves to see us fearful and depressed. Robbing us of our joy and serenity is his favorite activity.

Like David and my friend from church, children are also sur-rounded by foes against which they feel powerless and helpless. As a Lutheran schoolteacher, I enjoyed teaching my second grad-ers to sing "A Mighty Fortress Is Our God" each October as we talked about Martin Luther and the Reformation. As young chil-dren love to do, we acted out motions to the hymn—teeth-chatter-ing, nail-biting fear, for example, at the mention of "the old satanic foe" in stanza 1. Their favorite part of the hymn, and mine, was fist-pumping cheers accompanying these words in stanza 2: "But now a champion comes to fight, Whom God Himself elected. . . . He holds the field victorious." Like fans at a Friday night football game, they cheered Christ the victor as if He had just thrown the game-winning touchdown pass. I found that such efforts helped when bad news touched the lives of my students. We could talk about our fears and our foes and where to take them. Luke's class-mates listened as he shared his sadness when his parents sepa-rated and divorced. They grieved when Joy's grandfather passed away. We left those hurts and many others at the throne of grace in our prayers.

Because you and I are children, not strangers, of the Creator of the universe, we pray with confidence, "Deliver us from evil." Because we know the final score, we call upon our God and tell Him our troubles since we know He always listens. Because David knew where to take his problems, he was delivered from his son's betrayal—not by his own strength, but by God's power. You and I can laugh in the face of our foes rather than listen to their taunts

Judith

because we know that Christ is the victor for us. We are eternally connected to Him and to His victory over death and hell through our Baptism. On the cross, our champion endured the taunts and threats of His enemies on our behalf. He *is* our mighty fortress, our sword and shield victorious!

Prayer: We praise You, Lord, that You are our security—our fortress and safe place—in a world that often frightens us. In You alone we find peace and serenity because through Christ's death and resurrection, You have defeated all our foes. We pray this in Jesus' name. Amen.

Judith

monday

Personal Study Questions
Psalm 3:1–2

Read all of Psalm 3 to catch the context of the first two verses.

1. King David wrote Psalm 3 as he fled from Absalom, one of his own sons, who had hatched a treasonous plot to dethrone David. (See 2 Samuel 15–19.) With that as context, to what human foes might David be referring in verses 1–2?

2. Consider that the Lord had promised to send the Savior as David's descendant (2 Samuel 7). To what unearthly foes might these verses, then, also refer?

3. How would you characterize David's emotional state as he begins to pray? When have you felt something like that?

4. Worst of all, David hears the lie that "there is no salvation for him in God" (v. 2). Who might you suspect is telling this lie? When do you most often hear this discouraging refrain yourself? How do you know it is untrue?

Judith

Psalm 3:3–4

*But You, O Lord, are a shield about me, my glory,
and the lifter of my head. I cried aloud to the Lord,
and He answered me from His holy hill. Selah*

Prayer Shield

None of us likes to think of herself as helpless. As a nation, we value individualism and self-sufficiency. We boast of military strength and missile shields, and we like to think we can protect ourselves from just about any danger. As individuals, we chew calcium, pop vitamins, and slather on sunblock. We protect our children from measles, our homes from termites, our pets from fleas, and our lawns from weeds. My husband and I have car insurance, life insurance, long-term-care policies, and protection from identity theft. We get flu shots and visit the dentist every six months. And

Judith

that's not all.

I use other shields as well. One of my favorites is busyness. I've discovered that busyness is a great place to hide from other people and offers a socially acceptable and effective strategy for keeping people at arm's length. If I'm really busy, perhaps I won't have to be inconvenienced by someone else's problems or risk getting my feelings hurt by allowing someone to get too close to me.

So why do I still feel so vulnerable to the vicissitudes of life? As a child, I learned that one way to stay out of trouble was to keep busy with homework or chores. Satan likes to convince me that my productivity defines my self-worth. He whispers that my house must be the cleanest and that my students must be the best behaved and that somehow my sins are worse than yours. He enjoys reminding me of past failures, and he chips away at my self-confidence by bringing up memories that can still make me wince. Soon I am hanging my head in shame.

David was familiar with these flaming arrows of the enemy. I can only imagine Satan's jeers: "*You*? The *king*? After what *you* did? Get serious!" Finding himself surrounded by a multitude of enemies and a chorus of demonic voices, David confidently called on the name of the Lord. Verse 4 tells us that he cried out "aloud," that is, *loudly,* not shyly, head down, kicking the dirt asking, "Um, Lord, if You're not too busy. . . ." Rather, David yelled "Help!" at the top of his lungs.

One rainy summer day when I was young, I was in the basement with my mother as she did the laundry on her ancient wringer washing machine. I was playing nearby and watching as she carefully fed the wet sheets through the wringer, checking, as they snaked out the other end, to be sure they ended up in the wicker basket and not on the concrete floor. She pinned the sheets to dry on the clotheslines that crisscrossed the far end of the basement. I had seen her do this a hundred times, and yet I would hear an occasional yelp as she accidentally caught her fingertips in the wringer. "It's not as easy as it looks," she'd explain with a sigh, sloughing off the pain with a quick shake of her hand.

On this day, with all of the hubris an eight-year-old can pos-

Judith

sess, I decided I would help her by putting the sheets through the wringer while she hung the others on the line. Lifting a wet sheet out of the rinse water, I threaded it carefully into the wringer, beaming with self-satisfaction that I'd heeded my mother's admonition and my fingers did not get caught. I became so absorbed, however, in watching the sheet come out the other side and land safely in the basket at my feet that my arm, swathed in cold, wet, pink percale, slid slowly into the wringer all the way up to the elbow.

Sometimes I still hang my head in shame over my sins and failures because I know they nailed my Savior to His cross. But I also know without a doubt that my sins and failures are gone— wiped clean by Jesus' death and resurrection. My Redeemer lives!

In a nanosecond, my mother was at my side, pressing the button to release the machine's grip on my arm. My screams brought my sister and her friends running from a block away and my father barreling down three flights from his upstairs office. A hurried trip to the emergency room showed no broken bones, but the bruising and swelling was a painful (and really ugly) reminder of my mistake and helplessness. I was sure I'd be in big trouble, but my mom kept telling me how thankful she was that she had been right there to help.

When we're in trouble and life spins out of control, we want help without delay. We want the rescue heroes to get there fast, lights flashing and sirens blaring. God is our first responder, the One who is always available, always on call. We need His help when we're in crisis, such as those lonely, dark times when Satan whispers his ugly lies: "You're no good. Remember the time you . . . ?" In those dark moments, God replies, "I have called you by name, you are Mine" (Isaiah 43:1).

Satan sneers, "Who could possibly love you? You're all alone in this." But God promises, "I will not leave you or forsake you" (Joshua 1:5).

Prayer is the armor and shield that protect us from Satan. Our prayers, hollered or whispered, bring God running.

As parents, we do our best to protect our children. We can

Judith

shield them and ourselves from lots of things, but the one big enemy none of us can beat on our own is death.

Our friends buried their eleven-year-old son last week. As you can imagine, it was an awful experience for them. Born with a rare congenital heart defect and a host of other health issues, Bobby received a heart transplant as a toddler. He outlived both the doctors' expectations and every actuarial chart imaginable for one so young and so sick.

At the funeral home, we looked at the scrapbooks and picture frames that filled the visitation room with photos of Bobby. As we talked with family members, neighbors, and some of Bobby's teachers, each mentioned Bobby's smile that "just lit up a room." Looking around, I saw that smile everywhere—Bobby grinning at Christmas and Bobby laughing with Mickey Mouse. But the photo I'll always remember was right next to the guest book— a poster-size image of Bobby crossing the finish line at a Special Olympics track meet two years earlier. With his arms raised in a victory salute that would have made Rocky Balboa proud, Bobby's face registered pure, unadulterated joy. The famous "Bobby smile" showed every tooth.

During the funeral service, Bobby's dad recounted (with incredible composure) that he had known for eleven years that every day with Bobby was a gift from God. He thanked God for choosing him to be Bobby's dad. He shared his prayers for his son, including the one that ultimately asked God to take Bobby peacefully to his heavenly home. He told the story of the Special Olympics track meet, how Bobby was so thrilled to be able to participate and be "just like the other boys." He said he wasn't sure, though, if the joy on Bobby's face was because he crossed the finish line or because he was running straight into the outstretched arms of his mother, who was standing next to the photographer.

That image of Bobby's Special Olympics victory will stay with me for a very long time. Like Bobby, I am surrounded by a great cloud of witnesses cheering me on (Hebrews 12:1). I claim victory over my foes because of Christ's victory. I can smile in the face of death because I know into whose arms I run. One day I

Judith

will receive the victor's crown of glory for running the race and pressing on "toward the goal for the prize of the upward call of God in Christ Jesus" (Philippians 3:14).

Sometimes I still hang my head in shame over my sins and failures because I know they nailed my Savior to His cross. But I also know without a doubt that my sins and failures are gone—wiped clean by Jesus' death and resurrection. My Redeemer lives! Because God made me His child in my Baptism, my Father hears my cries and comes running, just like all those years ago when my mom sprinted across the basement and came to my rescue right when I needed her help the most. In fact, even before I cry out, He's already there.

Prayer:

With my burden I begin:

Lord, remove this load of sin;

Let Thy blood, for sinners spilt,

Set my conscience free from guilt.

While I am a pilgrim here,

Let Thy love my spirit cheer;

As my guide, my guard, my friend,

Lead me to my journey's end. *(LSB 779:3, 5)*

Judith

tuesday

Personal Study Questions
Psalm 3:3–4

1. What word pictures from verses 3–4 or from today's faith narrative commenting on these verses especially encourage your heart?

2. David follows verses 1–2 with the word *Selah*. Likewise, he follows verses 3–4 with the same word. While no one knows for sure, some scholars believe the word refers to a musical interlude that would allow worshipers to pause and meditate on the thoughts just shared. In that sense, *Selah* may mean "Pause and think about this." If that is the case, what makes these parallel pauses appropriate?

3. How would it help you today to remember that your Savior-God surrounds you like a shield?

Judith

Psalm 3:5–6

*I lay down and slept; I woke again,
for the LORD sustained me. I will not be
afraid of many thousands of people who have
set themselves against me all around.*

How Do You Spell Stress?

I like refrigerator magnets. There are several on my refrigerator door right now anchoring photos, reminders, and notes. A tooth-shaped magnet keeps my dentist's phone number handy. Another, shaped like a paw, reminds me when the cat needs her shots. A couple of them express sentiments about friendship and faith, and a few are souvenirs from family vacations. One magnet that always makes me smile was a gift to my husband. It shows a 1950s-era photo of a man wearing his wife's apron and a smile, with the message "No husband was ever shot while doing the dishes."

Judith

28

Front and center, where I see it every time I open the freezer, is my favorite magnet, a gift from my best friend. It says simply, "Peace. It does not mean to be in a place where there is no noise, trouble or hard work. It means to be in the midst of those things and still be calm in your heart. (Author unknown.)" I think the unknown author of that thought must have been a student of the Psalms who understood "My help comes from the LORD, who made heaven and earth" (Psalm 121:2).

If you had trouble sleeping last night, you definitely were not alone. Scientists estimate that as many as one-third of Americans suffer from insomnia and spend approximately $2 billion each year on sleep drugs. Articles on getting a good night's rest appear in almost every consumer magazine. Everyone has an answer: try progressive muscle relaxation or deep abdominal breathing. Take a warm bath or sip hot herb tea. Have a positive outlook on life. Read, do needlework, or concentrate on a puzzle before bed. Clearly, tossing and turning has become big business!

My husband and I went through a turbulent time in our marriage when we experienced several transitions within a very short period of time. His landscaping company enjoyed a burst of unprecedented growth. He took on a new partner and expanded his operations and staff to keep pace with the business boom. We had three children in college and had recently moved into our dream house. Life was good!

Within the next two years, however, the construction industry balloon began to deflate as housing starts hit an all-time low. My husband split from his business partner, had cancer surgery, and experienced a cardiac episode that resulted in a pacemaker being implanted in his chest. One of our sons married and divorced within a twelve-month period. After much agonizing and countless doctors' consultations, I moved my mother out of her home to an assisted-living facility, sold her car, and endured her "How could you do this to me?" glares and tears.

As our financial picture grew bleak, I began tutoring students after school and working part time at the mall to supplement our income. At the same time, I was riding the emotional

Judith

29

roller coaster of the empty-nest syndrome and was experiencing premenopausal symptoms.

Life wasn't quite so good anymore. My husband and I both lost a lot of sleep as we worried about money. We wondered if we might lose our beautiful new home and if our savings would disappear. My husband dealt with the stress much differently than I did. He retreated behind the newspaper and zoned out in front of the television night after night with scotch and sports; I felt angry and abandoned, and I cried. Counseling, warm baths, and herbal tea offered only minimal, temporary relief. I felt like a hypocrite as I blithely reassured my second-grade students of God's care and protection and sang "Children of the Heavenly Father" (*LSB* 725) during our morning devotions while my stomach was in knots.

If the Lord sustains us, He provides all that we need; we lack nothing, not even the faith required to stare down our enemies. Faith is a gift of grace—one more thing we cannot get or do for ourselves.

As I read the Psalms, I wonder how many nights King David paced the floor of the palace. Even with sentinels and palace guards on duty 24/7, he faced danger and threats. Enemies—tens of thousands of them!—surrounded him. King David's words in verse 5 sound almost boastful, as though he might be saying, "I can sleep even when my life is totally out of control. I've found the secret!" How did he do it? How could he enjoy restful repose while knowing things were so bad that even his own son Absalom was out to get him?

King David testifies in Psalm 3:5 that he could sleep and awake "for the LORD sustained me." To sustain something is to supply and nourish it. If the Lord sustains us, He provides all that we need; we lack nothing, not even the faith required to stare down our enemies. Faith is a gift of grace—one more thing we cannot get or do for ourselves.

The prophet Isaiah speaks another word of promise to us: "You keep him in perfect peace whose mind is stayed on You, because he trusts in You" (Isaiah 26:3). If anyone's mind was steadfast, or firmly fixed in place, with trust in God, it was David's. His heart was in tune with his heavenly Father's will. David's faith

Judith

was unmovable and unshakable because he knew from whence his help came. Perhaps recalling God's previous interventions on his behalf sustained him with hope. I like to imagine David replaying the defeat of Goliath in his mind and, like teammates in the locker room after winning the game, smiling and high-fiving God. David discovered the secret that God's provision releases us from worry and care. He knew that relying on God's promises rather than his own strength brought victory. David's mind was steadfast in faith and trust in the midst of danger, while mine, at the height of our family's stressful time, bounced around like a pinball from one negative thought to another.

When I shared my fears with a caring, reassuring friend, she suggested I switch my quiet time from the early morning hours, when I often struggled to stay awake, to bedtime, when my anxieties were really ramped up. She was reminded, she said, of a foolish person who is late for an appointment and whose car has run out of gas right in front of a gas station. Rather than pulling into the station to fill up the tank, the fool frantically tries to push the car down the street to get to the appointment. I was a fool, I thought, for not partaking of the rich fuel of God's Word when I truly needed it. I had been running on empty for far too long. The psalms, my friend reminded me, are the Bible's prayer book and songbook, giving us words when we have none of our own. I've always had a few favorites, but I had never plumbed the rich depths of the verses. She introduced me to Psalm 16, one of her favorites and now one of mine, especially verse 8: "I have set the LORD always before me; because He is at my right hand, I shall not be shaken."

Reading the psalms, especially at bedtime, can bring great comfort to our troubled spirits as they testify to God's provision and deliverance in times of trouble. The psalms celebrate our gracious God's action in our lives. They offer utterances of prayer and praise when life leaves us speechless. Because they were written by real people who experienced real problems, they remain a relevant reminder that God never slumbers or sleeps, is always present, and is ever watchful (Psalm 121:4–5).

Judith

Sometimes things still keep me awake at night. At those times, I picture myself as a child safe in my heavenly Father's arms. I recall promises from His Word. "The LORD your God is in your midst, a mighty one who will save; He will rejoice over you with gladness; He will quiet you by His love; He will exult over you with loud singing" (Zephaniah 3:17). And, like a small child who drifts off peacefully, knowing her parents are right in the next room, I sleep.

Prayer: We praise You, Lord God, heavenly Father. We can cast our cares and anxieties on You because of Your great love and mercy for us. We thank You for Your angels who guard and protect us, and for Your Word that comforts us and reassures us of Your presence and peace. We pray this in Jesus' name. Amen.

Judith

wednesday

Personal Study Questions
Psalm 3:5–6

1. As the psalmist remembers God's protecting care, he calms down enough to relax and even sleep (v. 5). When has your Savior's presence and peace enabled you to sleep, even in a time of distress and trouble?

2. How do God's promises and a good night's sleep change David's perspective on his many foes? (Compare vv. 1–2 with v. 6.) When have you experienced that same change in perspective?

3. The author of today's faith narrative quotes Isaiah 6:3— "You keep him in perfect peace whose mind is stayed on You, because he trusts in You." When have you experienced "perfect peace"? With what challenges might this verse help you right now?

Judith

Psalm 3:7

Arise, O LORD! Save me, O my God!
For You strike all my enemies on the cheek;
You break the teeth of the wicked.

Inconvenient Storms

Psalm 3:7 brings to mind the story of Jesus calming the storm. Can you picture the scene? Suddenly, a squall brews on the Sea of Galilee (Lake of Gennesaret), and the disciples frantically begin to bail water while Jesus dozes. Finally, in desperation, no longer trusting in their buckets and prowess, they wake Him, shouting, "Save us, Lord; we are perishing" (Matthew 8:25).

Life's storms often come upon us suddenly, more like

Judith

tornadoes than hurricanes. With hurricanes, there is time to board up windows and buy bottled water. Tornadoes, however, often appear without warning and can leave a wide swath of destruction in their wake. Having lived near the ocean for more than a quarter of a century, I have seen the destructive power of storms and have witnessed colossal waves that chew up the beach and multimillion-dollar homes. I understand how even highly experienced fishermen, like those in the boat with Jesus that day, could feel so overwhelmed and powerless in the presence of nature's fury that they would cry out to God, "Arise! Deliver us!" What always amazes me when I read the account is their awareness that the One who could do something about their desperate situation was right there in the boat with them.

My older sister, DeeDee, sent me a birthday e-card this year with a note that included a few memories of childhood events. Thinking of the card still makes me smile. In it, she told me how much she liked being my big sister. The irony is that although she is three years older, my "big sister" is about five inches shorter.

She has always been petite, but size did not deter her from sticking up for me against the bully who lived downstairs from us when we were kids. This boy delighted in teasing me. He would approach me on the sidewalk in front of our house where I played and stick his fingers into my eyes. Then, when my hands flew to my face, he would hit me in the stomach! DeeDee would come running, ready to take him on with all 4 feet 11 inches of her stretched out to her full height. Then, with an arm around my shoulders, she would walk me safely home.

DeeDee fought all of the typical adolescent and teen battles with our parents, too, making my teen years a breeze compared to hers. I think our parents were so worn down by the time she left for college that as long as I didn't come home in a police car, they were content to pretty much leave me alone. I admired (still do) her spirit of adventure and her feistiness. So naturally, when I discovered the lump in my neck, just below my left ear, I picked up the phone and called DeeDee first.

At that time, I was pregnant with my daughter. My obstetri-

Judith

cian sent me immediately to an excellent surgeon who advised postponing surgery until the baby was born, both to avoid risk to the fetus and because he felt confident that the chances of it being something other than an enlarged lymph node were pretty slim. When my daughter was just a few weeks old, the surgeon removed the lump during a five-hour operation. It turned out that the tumor was malignant. Fueled by pregnancy hormones and time, it had spread its tentacles deep into my neck and up into my face. Removing the tumor required severing the seventh nerve, resulting in facial paralysis. Now, besides the shock of learning that I was a twenty-five-year-old cancer patient whose face would never be the same, I had to deal with the painful separation from my new baby daughter during my week-long hospital stay and the anxiety that cancerous cells might have passed to her. The reality soon hit that I would need help for a while to care for her. When my husband had to return to work, DeeDee packed up her four-year-old and came to stay with us while I recovered. DeeDee cooked and cleaned, diapered the baby, and cried with me.

Life's storms are unavoidable. Whether you and I find ourselves frantically paddling our canoes upstream or enjoying smooth sailing on a clear day, God's gift of faith in our Savior calms and assures us.

Wherever we are, Jesus is right there in the boat with us.

I'd like to say that I dealt with all of this bravely, but I didn't. I was terrified—and oh, so angry! I imagine that I experienced much of the same fear David felt as a young shepherd in the Judean hills, aware of wild animals and other dangers that lurked nearby, ready to gobble up a lamb or ewe. During checkups, I held my breath, waiting for the doctor's smile and nod before I allowed myself to exhale. In my darkest midnight fears, I questioned whether I'd see my daughter start kindergarten or if I'd be around for her wedding day. My immature faith was sorely tested. I found my mother's gentle, well-intentioned reminders of my confirmation verse—"And we know that for those who love God all things work together for good, for those who are called according to His purpose" (Romans 8:28)—more annoying than comforting. The same rage David expressed in Psalm 3:7 also consumed me.

Judith

In the thirty years since my cancer surgery, I have watched my daughter grow into a beautiful, healthy young woman. My faith experienced other tests over the years, and with each, my confirmation verse began making more sense. Like other storms we all endure, cancer reordered my priorities and was part of God's loving plan to shape me and grow my faith.

Through those times of testing, God has been calling me into the kind of intimate relationship He wants with each of us, the kind He enjoyed with His servant David. During those stormy times, we can say, with the Holy Spirit's help, "The Lord is my helper; I will not fear" (Hebrews 13:6), and understand that in all things, even the things we fear most, God works for the good of those who love Him.

Life's storms are unavoidable, but God's gift of faith in our Savior calms and assures us. Wherever we are, Jesus is right there in the boat with us. So put away your buckets, and rejoice that "even winds and sea obey Him" (Matthew 8:27).

Prayer: Thank You, Jesus, for promising to never leave us or forsake us, no matter what each day brings. Thank You for delivering us from our enemies. When life's storms make us angry and it seems that You are far away, strengthen our faith and reassure us with the promises in Your Word. Amen.

Judith

thursday

Personal Study Questions
Psalm 3:7

1. In verse 7, David echoes a liturgical refrain Moses prayed during Israel's wilderness wanderings. Whenever the priests picked up the ark of the covenant and set out on that day's journey, Moses would shout, "Arise, O LORD, and let Your enemies be scattered, and let those who hate You flee before You" (Numbers 10:35). Inspired by the Holy Spirit, David later incorporated these words into Israel's hymnal in both Psalm 3 and Psalm 68. Why might David have used these words at this point in Psalm 3?

2. With what words does David indicate his expectation that his enemies will be humiliated and suffer total defeat?

3. How do these words foreshadow Jesus' defeat of Satan at the cross?

4. How does the thought of Satan's total defeat and humiliation encourage you as you face today's challenges?

I know how it will end up;

like cont verse you hear it a lot it it be comes part of your faith response

Psalm 3:8

Salvation belongs to the LORD;
Your blessing be on Your people!
Selah

The Power of the Blessing

As a king of Israel, it was appropriate for David to offer public prayers on behalf of the people. The prayer spoken in Psalm 3:8 is first of all a statement of fact: "Salvation belongs to the LORD." It is David's acknowledgement of God's sovereignty and his confession that Yahweh alone works our redemption. God alone delivers us from evil and from the power of sin, death, and the devil.

David wrote this psalm as he was fleeing from

Absalom, so we might expect that he was not in a mood to bless anyone. Yet, his kingly prayer continues, and he speaks words of benediction, "good words," asking God to bless His people.

What do you think of when you hear the word *blessing*? Mealtime prayers? the pastor's hand on a child's head at the baptismal font? a hearty, well-meant "*Gesundheit*"?

Blessing means something very specific to God, who gave His covenant blessing to Abram (Genesis 12). God's blessing always conveys good things. Through the covenant, God established a relationship with those He chose as His people. The blessing was

David's benediction becomes our own statement of confidence that "He who began a good work in you will bring it to completion at the day of Jesus Christ" (Philippians 1:6).

to be passed on to Abram's descendants. "You will be a blessing," God said to Abram; "in you all the families of the earth shall be blessed" (Genesis 12:2–3). God's original blessing given to Adam and Eve (Genesis 1:28) would be restored. The promise would be fulfilled through God's chosen people. The relationship broken by sin would be reconciled through the redeeming work of God's chosen one, Jesus Christ.

A blessing is powerful. A parent's blessing communicates love and acceptance and points a child toward a secure future. In Old Testament times, bestowing the blessing and birthright on a child, as Abraham did with Isaac, affirmed the child's identity and place in the family. It also included the aspect of inheritance. Firstborn males received a double portion of the family's wealth and assumed the responsibility of being the family's leader and caretaker. No wonder Esau was devastated when he lost both his birthright *and* his blessing to his sneaky, scheming brother, Jacob! Coming to his father after Isaac had already spoken the blessing to Jacob, Esau desperately lamented, "Have you but one blessing, my father? Bless me, even me also, O my father" (Genesis 27:38).

Every family has stories told, sometimes, with a shake of the head or a chuckle. Which stories do you recall? Perhaps as a youngster you heard about an uncle whose get-rich-quick schemes resulted in bankruptcy or about a cousin who broke her parents'

hearts when she eloped. The story I had always heard about my father's family was that they were so very German they never hugged—they saluted.

Some stories are told to remind us of the family heroes whose victories and successes cause us to swell with pride. Fred, my paternal great-grandfather, settled in Cleveland, Ohio, and, after a humble start laying sidewalks, became a wealthy contractor who built many homes on Cleveland's West Side. I recall walking with my mother along the streets near historic old Trinity Lutheran Church on West 29th and seeing our family name branded into the sidewalks. There is even a nearby street named after him! You can imagine how proud I felt as a child to enjoy such notoriety and be part of such a family.

My father inherited his father's blue eyes and bad temper but none of Grandpa Fred's money. Following a bitter argument over who knows what, my father's mother disinherited him and gave his share of the family's wealth to his unmarried sister, my Aunt Anne. Betrayed and angry, my father never reconciled with either of them. But my sister and I dutifully maintained contact with our elderly aunt—mostly through greeting cards and holiday phone calls—even after our father passed away. So it came as a shock to receive a letter one day from an attorney informing me that Aunt Anne had died two months earlier. In her will, my aunt acknowledged that we were her rightful heirs, but stipulated that we were to receive nothing, not even the family photos. She left her entire estate to a friend.

As I struggled to make sense of it, I realized that I wasn't upset about the money; it was that my sister and I were experiencing the consequences of a relationship that had been broken thirty years earlier. Like Esau, I yearned for some sort of blessing from my aunt, some kind word of acknowledgement that I was part of the family I was so proud of.

The irony of blessing is that while we are always on the receiving end of blessings with God, we are also called to bless His holy name (Psalm 103:1). How can we bless God's name when we, like David, come to Him helpless and empty-handed? God's name

Judith

describes His character; blessing God's name blesses Him and acknowledges that deliverance comes from Him alone. Praising God's holy name acknowledges that He is the King and we are not. Perhaps that is exactly the point. When we admit our powerlessness and believe unequivocally that apart from Him, we can do nothing, we are exactly where God wants us to be. Laying down our pitiful weapons and admitting "I can't; God can" is the way for us to bless His holy name.

The Psalms are full of statements of confidence that God has heard the prayer offered by the writer. David's prayer for God's blessing to be on His people was heard and answered in the person of Jesus Christ. David's benediction becomes our own statement of confidence that "He who began a good work in you will bring it to completion at the day of Jesus Christ" (Philippians 1:6).

Although my father's family ultimately denied me both a blessing and an inheritance, I joyfully claim both as a member of my heavenly Father's family through my Baptism. Because of our place in the family as children of the King with Christ as our Brother, we know to whom we belong and that we will be with Him one day. Because of our heavenly Father's blessing, we can say with confidence, "The LORD is my chosen portion and my cup; You hold my lot. The lines have fallen for me in pleasant places; indeed, I have a beautiful inheritance" (Psalm 16:5–6).

Prayer: Father, our families may disappoint and hurt us, but You never do! Help us to forgive as You have forgiven us in Christ, our Lord. Remind us daily of our delightful inheritance, made ours through Baptism. You have made us Your own and have blessed us so we may be a blessing to others. We ask this in Jesus' name. Amen.

Judith

Friday

Personal Study Questions
Psalm 3:8

1. Like all the psalms in this volume, Psalm 3 falls into the category many scholars have termed "Psalms of Lament." The psalm starts out that way, but it certainly does not end in lamentation. What contrasts do you see between verses 1–2 and verse 8? *Major change in focus! Probably major change in feelings, as well.*

2. Note the psalm's third *Selah* as verse 8 ends. What makes this opportunity for meditation appropriate, comforting, and helpful for you as you consider the things that provoke lamentations in your own heart today? *This is the ultimate conclusion, even when things are rocky.*

3. Today's faith narrative highlights several aspects of "the blessing" that make it a powerful influence on our lives. Which of these have you received from your family of origin? Which have you received from your heavenly Father? How has God's blessing, in this sense, changed your life?

Approval, acceptance, love from family; God's good will, guidance, presence, help, victory!

Judith

Group Bible Study for Week 1
Psalm 3

1. This week's faith narratives included many poignant stories that served to illustrate the psalmist's meaning and connect it with our lives today. Which faith narrative did you find especially helpful or meaningful? Explain.

2. Scholars often categorize Psalm 3 as a "Psalm of Lament." What characteristics probably led to this categorization?

3. Consider the picture of God the psalm paints.

   a. How would you describe that picture?

   b. When might returning to this picture help you in your own times of lamentation?

4. Psalm 3 incorporates the term *Selah* three times. Why might each placement of the term provide an ideal opportunity to pause for thought and prayer?

5. As verse 3 begins, the psalm pivots sharply and moves in exactly the opposite direction.

    a. What leads to the "but" that begins verse 3?

    b. What most often leads to the "but" in times of lamentation—the "but" that turns your own heart from fear to faith?

6. Think about your time in God's Word this week, and consider the faith narratives you have read.

    a. How has all this changed you?

    b. What new insights have you gained?

    c. What people, events, challenges, and opportunities do you see differently?

    d. What would you like to say to God about any or all of this?

Week Two

Psalm 4

[1] Answer me when I call, O God of my righteousness!
You have given me relief when I was in distress.
Be gracious to me and hear my prayer!

[2] O men, how long shall my honor be turned into shame?
How long will you love vain words and seek after lies? *Selah*

[3] But know that the LORD has set apart the godly for Himself;
the LORD hears when I call to Him.

[4] Be angry, and do not sin;
ponder in your own hearts on your beds, and be silent. *Selah*

[5] Offer right sacrifices,
and put your trust in the LORD.

[6] There are many who say, "Who will show us some good?
Lift up the light of Your face upon us, O LORD!"

[7] You have put more joy in my heart
than they have when their grain and wine abound.

[8] In peace I will both lie down and sleep;
for You alone, O LORD, make me dwell in safety.

Jane Wilke

Psalm 4:1–2

Answer me when I call, O God of my righteousness!
You have given me relief when I was in distress. Be gracious to me
and hear my prayer! O men, how long shall my honor be turned into
shame? How long will you love vain words and seek after lies? Selah

Shift Happens

I live in St. Louis, Missouri. The summers are close to unbearable because of the heat and humidity, but the rest of the seasons make up for it: spring is gorgeous with its blooms, autumn has more days that qualify as Indian summer than not, and winter is, well, winter, but it's usually on the mild side. When visitors come to town, they are never at a loss for things to do.

The zoo is free, the botanical gardens are outstanding, and there are more species of butterflies in the butterfly garden than I knew even existed. But best of all, there is the St. Louis Gateway Arch.

The Arch (the shortened name as we all call it) is a truly magnificent structure. It stands on the banks of the mighty Mississippi River and is built on the grounds of the Jefferson National Expansion Memorial Park. Its gleaming exterior, made completely of stainless steel, spans 630 feet at ground level and rises 630 feet in the air. Sitting on its steps on the Fourth of July, you can be treated to one of the most incredible fireworks displays found anywhere. And when you stand under the Arch and look up, you can barely see the windows at the top. Who wouldn't want to travel to the top in one of the trams that goes up the Arch's legs to peer out those windows and see for miles?

That's what I thought. After moving here, I couldn't wait for that first opportunity to "go to the top of the Arch." We bought our tickets and stood in line, listening to the park ranger (it's a national park) as we waited. Once the tram doors opened, we were ushered into one of the cramped, tubular compartments. Shoulder to shoulder, the five of us passengers watched the doors close and readied ourselves for the trip to the top.

No one talked except to comment on the close quarters. We simply sat and waited as we felt the car moving upward. Then it happened—the jerk, accompanied by a loud, creaking, groaning sound. We nervously looked at one another, not wanting to shout "What's happening? Are we going down?" But then it happened again . . . and again . . . and again. We later discovered that if we had listened to that park ranger a bit more closely, we would have learned that to keep us perpendicular to the ground as we moved upward, the tram cars had to shift several times along the way.

In other words, we would have known that "shift happens," and when it does, it's for a purpose—and it's okay.

Shift happens in life, too, doesn't it? We are cruising along with everything to look forward to and then it happens—some sort of jerk, accompanied by loud creaks and groans. And not just once, but time and time again. Our first reaction is to cry out,

Sane

"What's happening? Are we going down?"

That's not unlike what we find in the cries of David in the first verse of Psalm 4. Some writers of commentaries say this psalm was written while David was being pursued by Saul, fearing for his very life. Others say it was written during some sort of calamity, such as drought. But no matter what the circumstances, it is clearly a prayer for deliverance from some sort of distress.

When difficulties, disappointments, dead ends, and despair come our way, we need to remember that it's not the shift itself that matters, but how God can use it to bring us closer to Him and to teach us to trust Him.

I can relate. Can you? The shifts in our lives come in all shapes and sizes, from disappointments and difficulties to dead ends and despair. Whether they have to do with relationships or jobs, health or family, they often turn into crises. We find ourselves standing like deer in the headlights, frozen in place, staring helplessly. And all the while, life keeps rushing at us. What's happening? Am I going down? What do I do now? Well, what did David do? He turned his troubles over to the Lord with confidence that his prayers would be answered.

Turning our troubles over to the Lord is a recurring theme throughout the Bible. In Psalm 55:22, David writes, "Cast your burden on the LORD, and He will sustain you; He will never permit the righteous to be moved." Our Lord and Savior, Jesus Christ, tells us in Matthew 11:28: "Come to Me, all who labor and are heavy laden, and I will give you rest." And in 1 Peter 5:7, we read these words from the apostle Peter as he writes and encourages new believers: "[Cast] all your anxieties on Him, because He cares for you."

You might find yourself wondering if these are empty promises, words that hold no meaning. But they are far from empty. Why? Because of two words in this first verse of David's psalm: *righteousness* and *gracious*.

Righteousness. David describes God as righteous throughout his psalms as he makes reference to the faithfulness of God. Keep in mind that at this time in Old Testament history, God had made a covenant of love with His people. He was their divine King, the one to whom the powerless could look for protection. It is no dif-

Sane

50

ferent for us; God has also made a covenant of love with us. It is sealed in our Baptism and its conditions are met through Christ Jesus Himself.

Yes, it's true . . . shift happens. Plain and simple, shift happens because of sin, and sin is part of our lives. We cannot escape the pain and brokenness sin brings, but God in His faithfulness has prepared a way to escape its consequence of eternal punishment. He sent His very Son, Jesus Christ, to die on the cross of Calvary for our sins. In victory over sin, Jesus rose from death in order to secure forgiveness for our sins and a place in His eternal kingdom for all who believe in Him as Savior. He is our King, and although we are powerless over sin, we can look to Him for forgiveness, protection, and power to withstand whatever shifts sin brings our way.

Gracious. The simple definition of *grace* is not receiving what we deserve. David prays that God would be gracious to him in his time of need. That prayer becomes ours every time we acknowledge that as long as we live on this side of heaven, we cannot escape the shifts in life that sin brings. But God is a loving God—He made the world and all that is in it. We can be assured that God in His grace does indeed forgive our sins for Jesus' sake and that nothing will ever happen to us that God does not know about or care about.

Remember my reference to the shifts in the tram while going to the top of the Arch? They happened for a reason—to keep us level along the way. There's something we can take away from that: God can use every shift in our lives for His purposes. When difficulties, disappointments, dead ends, and despair come our way, we need to remember that it's not the shift itself that matters, but how God can use it to bring us closer to Him and to teach us to trust Him.

The apostle Paul had a face-to-face encounter with Jesus, and he dedicated the rest of his life to bringing the Good News of God's love for us in Christ to others. Yet, he was not without his own shifts in life. He was thrown into prison on more than one occasion because of his faith, and he made reference to some sort

Sane

of "thorn . . . in the flesh" (2 Corinthians 12:7) that remained although he asked God to remove it. Despite all this, he wrote these words with all confidence:

Rejoice in the Lord always; again I will say, Rejoice. . . . The Lord is at hand; do not be anxious about anything, but in everything by prayer and supplication with thanksgiving let your requests be made known to God. And the peace of God, which surpasses all understanding, will guard your hearts and your minds in Christ Jesus. Philippians 4:4–7

Note to self: shift happens. Second note to self: call upon God in the time of trouble for He will deliver me (see Psalm 91:15). What can be better than that?

Prayer: Dear God, heavenly Father, there are times when my faith is so small that I forget to look to You. Teach me to come to You in times of trouble, trusting in Your wisdom and in Your love to see me through. In the name of Jesus, Your Son, my Savior, I pray. **Amen.**

Sane

monday

Personal Study Questions
Psalm 4:1–2

1. Skim through Psalm 4. What evidence seems to make this a "Psalm of Lament" like Psalm 3? *V 1, V2, V6*

2. Verse 1 reads as though David had just run into God's throne room and, breathless, had begun to scream out his need. When have you been caught up in such distress that you ran to your Lord with similar words of fear and desperation?

3. The first sentence could sound like a demand. But with what words does the psalmist acknowledge that he cannot demand anything from God, that he deserves nothing but punishment?

4. In what situations in your life today is "shift" happening? From what distress do you need relief from your Savior-God today? Because of His righteousness and mercy, you can count on His help! What will you ask Him to do?

① V1: Calling for help, in distress
  r2 honor to shame; men loving vain words
  V6: "who will show us some good?"
   - Asking for God's face
② When I'm scared by my own inability
   to handle temptation; worried about
   Dan;
③ Be gracious to me - I don't deserve this
④ Eating habits; work; relationships; Dan
   Yes! Guide, strengthen, keep my eyes
   fixed on Jesus

Sane

53

Psalm 4:3–4

*But know that the LORD has set apart the godly for Himself;
the LORD hears when I call to Him. Be angry, and do not sin;
ponder in your own hearts on your beds, and be silent. Selah*

The Definition of Insanity

It's been said that the definition of insanity is doing the same thing over and over and expecting different results. Now, I don't know for sure who said it; I've found it attributed to Benjamin Franklin, Albert Einstein, and Mark Twain. But it doesn't matter who said it. It's what was said that counts.

I can think of various examples of insanity in my own life. For starters, I'm a redhead with very fair skin. Exposure to sunlight has always led to sunburn. Worse yet, my skin goes from bright red right back to pasty white—never bronzed or tan, always bright red or

Sane

54

pasty white. Yet, for some reason I can attribute only to insanity, every summer when I was growing up, I would put on my bathing suit to lie in the sun to "get a tan." Was it good for me? No. Did I ever learn? Gratefully, yes.

Consider also my daily chocolate fix. Somehow I keep thinking that I'll drop those last ten pounds even though I keep giving in to my cravings for chocolate. Have I not yet figured out if I keep eating one . . . or two . . . or three pieces of chocolate, those pounds will be with me forever? Have I never heard that just one moment on my lips means a lifetime on my hips?

As we take a closer look at the second and third verses of Psalm 4, we see David posing some important questions to those around him who have turned from God. "How long," he asks, "shall my honor be turned into shame? How long will you love vain words and seek after lies?" (v. 2). David could be asking the same question of us. How long will we keep falling into the same trap, believing the same lies, doing the same harmful things over and over again? I'm not talking about minor things like deluding myself into thinking I'd actually get a suntan or that the calories in chocolate don't count. I'm talking about the much more serious issues of insanity. I'm talking about looking to the wrong things in life—placing our trust in false gods over and over again and expecting things to somehow be different, even better.

You may think this doesn't apply to you; after all, you don't follow any false gods, do you?

I'm reminded of a story about some zoologists who went into the jungle to capture monkeys. They tried many methods, but the monkeys were quick and clever and avoided capture. Finally, the scientists happened upon an ingenious solution. They made several small, wooden boxes. Into the top of each box, they bored a hole just large enough for a monkey to insert its hand. In each box they placed a nut. They then set out the boxes under the trees. After the scientists left, the curious monkeys came down from the trees to examine the boxes. One by one, as each monkey discovered the treat inside, it would reach through the hole to retrieve the nut. Holding it tightly, the monkey would try to withdraw its

Sane

hand, only to discover that his little fist with the nut inside was too large to pull out through the hole. That's when the zoologists reappeared. The monkeys scrambled about, trying to escape. But because they would not let go of the nuts to withdraw their hands from the boxes, the monkeys were easily captured.

Now, back to you and me and false gods. False gods are those things in which we place our trust more than in God Himself—pride, vanity, money, possessions. In so doing, we seek the fast track to happiness on our own terms. This could be referred to as "self-anity"; it becomes insanity when we keep going after such things, holding them in our hot little fists, expecting them to finally satisfy, when all they really do is disappoint.

While the world might consider it insanity to hope in the Lord, those of us who walk as both saint and sinner, living in the assurance that we are forgiven and redeemed in the blood of Christ, know that His mercies are new every morning.

David saw that those who turned their backs on God were seeking happiness and fulfillment in fruitless efforts. He asked, "Why do you keep doing the same things over and over, expecting the results to be different, expecting to suddenly find what you are looking for?" He could have been tempted to give up and turn his back on them, but he didn't.

He stepped out in courage, although the others likely considered him—not themselves—to be the definition of insanity. After all, didn't he keep relying on and praying to God even when things weren't going well? Didn't he keep doing the same thing over and over, expecting different results?

The word *courage* comes from the Latin word for *heart*, which is to say that courage is born in the heart. It took great courage to stand up to those who thought he was insane for trusting in God. But deep in his heart, David knew he was one of God's chosen; he had been set apart to be devoted to God out of gratitude for God's faithfulness to him.

Cannot—should not—the same be said of us? According to the world's definition, it would be insane to trust in God (whom we cannot see) to hear us and answer. The world thinks we keep praying and praying, expecting the results to be different. What

Sane

they don't realize is that every time we pray, the same thing does indeed happen: God hears us and He answers.

We have only to look to the Bible to find evidence of God's commitment and faithfulness to those who wavered between trusting in Him and trusting in other gods. How about the children of Israel, who started worshiping a golden calf while Moses, their leader, was on the mountain, conversing with the very God who had faithfully delivered them from the clutches of mighty Pharaoh? How about the prophets of the Old Testament, who continually warned God's people not to turn their backs on Him, only to witness the heartbreak of ruin and eventual captivity?

Jeremiah was one of those prophets. In his words, we see heartbreak, and yet he also offers a ringing testimony to God's faithfulness and goodness. Although the present looks bleak, the future is bright with the promise of renewal and restoration. Consider these words of Jeremiah:

> *My soul is bereft of peace; I have forgotten what happiness is; so I say, "My endurance has perished; so has my hope from the LORD." . . . But this I call to mind, and therefore I have hope: The steadfast love of the LORD never ceases; His mercies never come to an end; they are new every morning; great is Your faithfulness. . . . The LORD is good to those who wait for Him, to the soul who seeks Him. It is good that one should wait quietly for the salvation of the LORD.* Lamentations 3:17–18, 21–26

There it is, pure and simple: while the world might consider it insanity to hope in the Lord, those of us who walk as both saint and sinner, living in the assurance that we are forgiven and redeemed in the blood of Christ, know that His mercies are new every morning. That's a definition of insanity I can live with!

Sane

Prayer: Dear Father, You are ever faithful despite the times I cling to other things rather than You. Forgive me and teach me to pray so I might look to You only as the source of lasting hope. In Jesus' name. **Amen.**

tuesday

Personal Study Questions
Psalm 4:3–4

1. Today's faith narrative focuses on the insanity of idolatry. We know this sin hurts us, yet we cling tightly to our idols anyway. To which false gods do you customarily turn in times of trouble? What kinds of results do you expect to receive? What do you want to say to your Lord about all this?

2. What contrasts do you see between verses 2 and 3?

3. Just think of it! The Lord has "set you apart" for Himself! His protecting love is "a shield about [you]" (Psalm 3:3). Jesus' cross shields you from the destructive power of your sins, and His blood washes away your guilt. How does the Lord's special favor encourage you, even as you lament today?

1. - Food! - Instant comfort
   - Distraction -   "
   False Gods in times of peace are perhaps a bigger problem!

2. Faith in false things vs God
   v 2 No mention of God
   v 3 ALL about Him

3. I know if I lose focus & stray, He ALWAYs is there and that 'He has' all of this in His control, working on me through it.

Sane

Psalm 4:5

*Offer right sacrifices,
and put your trust in the LORD.*

Transformed

I recently met an eighty-one-year-old woman who has led a fascinating life. She is a mother of five and a grandmother of many, and more than that, she is a civic reformer—it was through her tenacity and foresight that an entire neighborhood was reborn.

Years earlier, her husband had died and she was left to raise their five children. She had few resources but a lot of faith. Against the wishes of those who knew her, she used what little money she had to buy a house on a street that wove itself as a square around a large park. At one time, the street had been bustling with activity, but the activity had long since ceased, and the house, like the others around it, had been left in

Sane

ruins. The most activity it had seen recently was from the rodents and roaches that now called it home. But this did not dissuade her—she was on a mission to transform what was old into something new.

And transform it she did. It took several years and the labor of many, but the square and the park have since been restored to a place of beautiful, historic, Victorian-era homes.

To be transformed means to be changed from one state of being into another. A different example of transformation is that of a caterpillar being transformed into a beautiful butterfly. I was a teacher for many years, and curious children brought in many caterpillars. We would place them in the obligatory jar with holes punched in the lid. We'd line the bottom of the jar with leaves and balance a twig or small stick against the side. Then we'd watch as the caterpillar spun its cocoon, and we'd wait until the butterfly emerged. I remember with great clarity one time in particular when a monarch butterfly emerged from a picture-perfect chrysalis. I still marvel at the miracle of transformation.

In the verses we studied yesterday (Psalm 4:3–4), David speaks of transformation. He begins in verse 4 by urging those around him not to give in to the intensity of their emotions and not to act rashly in the heat of the moment. We do not know what sort of distress surrounded them, but it was enough to create anxiety and fear, even anger.

We've all experienced anger; it's at the root of many emotions. It is so very basic that much has been written about how to control anger before it controls us. We've all felt it, whether simply as a fleeting annoyance or as a full-fledged rage. It's a completely normal, usually healthy emotion; but when it gets out of control, it can most certainly turn destructive, hurting others and hurting ourselves.

It would seem that David is referring here to the sort of anger that is born of exasperation. Whatever is going on, it appears to have existed for a while. He could be urging them to not act out in anger toward one another, but perhaps he is urging them to not act out in anger toward God.

Have you ever been angry at God, exasperated with a circumstance that seems out of control? angry that God doesn't seem to be doing anything?

Off the coast of Maine, a Navy ship was sailing in very dense fog. The midshipman saw a fixed light in the distance and immediately contacted his captain. Worried, he asked, "There's a light in the distance heading straight for us. What do you want me to do?" The captain told him to flash a signal to the vessel, directing it to change course. They received the signal back: "No, *you* change *your* course." Once again, the captain instructed the midshipman to command the oncoming vessel to change its course immediately. Again the reply was, "No, *you* change *your* course." Making one last attempt, the midshipman signaled the vessel, saying, "This is the captain of a U.S. Navy battleship, and you are to change your course immediately."

He received this reply: "No, *you* change *your* course. This is a lighthouse."

In our silent reflection, we come to realize once again that Jesus suffered the ultimate rejection that we deserved, and He did it willingly for us as a sacrifice for our sins. In repentance, we are transformed. The old becomes new.

Isn't that how we as sinful human beings tend to deal with exasperation, questions, pain, and suffering? We want the circumstances to change course rather than allowing ourselves to be changed to meet those circumstances. But such a change would most certainly require a transformation, one that is well beyond our control.

Helen Keller, an inspiration as she lived each day both blind and deaf, referred to character as something that cannot be developed in ease and quiet. Rather, she felt that it was only through the experience of trial and suffering that the soul can be strengthened. I wonder if she was ever angry at God about the circumstances of her life. Yet she clearly became someone who didn't live "under" the circumstances; instead, she lived "above" them.

But how, you may ask, does anger get transformed into hope? In verses 3–4, David urges the exasperated to go to their beds. search their hearts, and to be silent. Now in verse 5 he tells them

to offer the right kind of sacrifices by trusting in the Lord.

It sounds to me as if David is urging them toward repentance and faith. The same is true for us—no type of real, true transformation can come about because of our own actions. As we consider the many times we have come face-to-face with our emotions and have given in to acting upon them in ways that hurt others or ourselves, we have actually come face-to-face with the reality of our own sin. We want to give excuses, but in our silence, we know we are wrong.

In searching our hearts, we realize that we often feel tired and disillusioned. That's nothing unique to us; we need only to read through the psalms to be reminded that David often felt the same. In Psalm 22:1, he writes, "My God, my God, why have You forsaken me? Why are You so far from saving me, from the words of my groaning?"

It's interesting that Jesus Christ, our Savior, uttered those very words from the cross when He said, "'Eli, Eli, lema sabachthani?' that is, 'My God, My God, why have You forsaken Me?'" (Matthew 27:46). In our silent reflection, we come to realize once again that Jesus suffered the ultimate rejection that we deserved, and He did it willingly for us as a sacrifice for our sins. In repentance and faith, we are transformed. The old becomes new: "Therefore, if anyone is in Christ, he is a new creation. The old has passed away; behold, the new has come" (2 Corinthians 5:17).

So, what can we do in return? In the Old Testament, God required that sacrifices be offered for the forgiveness of sins. Christ became the ultimate sacrifice for us, and because of His sacrifice on our behalf, we have been reconciled to God our Father. There is nothing we need to do or can do to win forgiveness and salvation; it's already been done. What we do in return is not done to gain favor but to give thanks. We have been transformed from sinful creatures into a new creation, and now our lives can become living sacrifices of gratitude: "And [Christ] died for all, that those who live might no longer live for themselves but for Him who for their sake died and was raised" (2 Corinthians 5:15).

Going back to David and our psalm, we see that he told those around him to offer right sacrifices and to trust in God. It's time to take our everyday, ordinary lives of sleeping, eating, working, raising families, and simply walking around and place them before God as our offering. In his letter to the Romans, the apostle Paul writes,

> *I appeal to you, therefore, brothers, by the mercies of God, to present your bodies as a living sacrifice, holy and acceptable to God, which is your spiritual worship. Do not be conformed to this world, but be transformed by the renewal of your mind, that by testing you may discern what is the will of God, what is good and acceptable and perfect.* Romans 12:1–2

We are transformed—from the old to the new. Let's live like we believe it!

Prayer: "Heal me, O Lord, and I shall be healed; save me, and I shall be saved, for You are my praise" (Jeremiah 17:14). In the name of Jesus, I pray. **Amen.**

Sane

Personal Study Questions
Psalm 4:5

1. As we lie in silence, perhaps even sleepless because of our distress and anger (v. 4), we ponder our Lord's goodness to us, His care for us. Through David's prophetic words, the Holy Spirit also urges us to "offer right sacrifices." Consider Psalm 51:17. What are these right sacrifices?

2. Which examples of transformation from today's faith narrative mean most to you? Explain.

3. Today's faith narrative ends with this statement of hope, followed by a challenge: "We are transformed—from the old to the new. Let's live like we believe it!" What would that kind of transformed life look like in your activities and relationships today?

Sane

Psalm 4:6–7

There are many who say, "Who will show us some good?
Lift up the light of Your face upon us,
O LORD!" You have put more joy in my heart than
they have when their grain and wine abound.

It's All About Perspective

Paper or plastic? Debit or credit? Half empty or half full? These are our choices on a daily basis. The first two probably sound familiar, but what about the third? We do have the choice to see every situation as a pessimist (half empty) or an optimist (half full). It's all about perspective.

A few years ago, I started a new position. Only a month or two into my job, my boss was diagnosed with amyotrophic lateral sclerosis (ALS), commonly called "Lou Gehrig's disease." If you are not familiar with it, I can tell

you without exaggeration that it is devastating. It's a progressive neurodegenerative disease that affects nerve cells in the brain and spinal cord. As motor neurons die, the brain's ability to initiate and control muscle movement is lost. The muscles atrophy, and in the later stages, it can lead to paralysis. In effect, you become trapped in your own body. Your brain still functions with all capacity to think, but the rest of your body shuts down.

My boss lived with this disease for two years before a respiratory failure ushered him to heaven. To watch this disease ravage this man in his early forties was sobering, to say the least. At the same time, however, it was also an inspiration, for this man of faith never lost his perspective. It must have been a struggle beyond description to face each day with peace in his heart, but he was able to do just that. How? Not by relying on his own strength, but by tapping into the peace that was his through faith in Christ. He chose to focus not on the agony but, instead, on hope. Although it was heartbreakingly slow for him to nudge the joystick of a computer that talked for him, he never lost an opportunity to share his conviction that this disease would not defeat him because he had an eternity in heaven with Christ waiting for him.

Half empty or half full? It's all about perspective!

In Psalm 4, we see David praying for God to bless those around him who seek happiness from the outward trappings of what they consider "good." They seek happiness, but interestingly enough, David himself has found it. And he prays that the light of God's face might shine upon them so they, too, can find it. Perhaps these words remind you of the benediction pastors often use as they lift their hands to bless the congregation. The words are found in Numbers 6:24–26: "The LORD bless you and keep you; the LORD make His face to shine upon you and be gracious to you; the LORD lift up His countenance upon you and give you peace."

To ask that God lift up His countenance upon us is to ask for the blessing that can be ours only because He does not frown upon our sins; rather, the beams of forgiveness stream down from Him to us. To ask that God look upon us with favor is to ask that because of His grace, He not see our sins but instead, smile upon us and grant us His peace. The Hebrew word for "peace" in these verses is *shalom*, which does not mean the absence of conflict or war but a sense of harmonious oneness that is centered in God. Despite trouble in our lives, we can experience the very mysterious peace that comes only from God, resulting in well-being and wholeness—in other words, perspective.

This is a pretty generous prayer that David offers up for those who believe happiness to be found in the people and things they can see rather than in God. David, on the other hand, has discovered that lasting happiness is found only in the character of God and the gift of His grace. He confesses joyfully that despite the various troubles he experiences, God has never let him down. His troubles are transformed into an inner sense of divine grace that far surpasses the happiness others find in the material blessings of a bountiful harvest of grain and wine. And he wants, more than anything, for them to experience this peace, this happiness, this joy, as well.

David discovered that lasting happiness is found only in the character of God and the gift of His grace. He confesses joyfully that despite the various troubles he experiences, God has never let him down.

How about us? We need only to look in the Book of Philippians to find the peace that manifests itself in real, true, lasting joy. The apostle Paul opens this letter of encouragement with these words: "I thank my God in all my remembrance of you, always in every prayer of mine for you all making my prayer with joy, because of your partnership in the gospel" (1:3–5). Do you sense the joy? A few verses later, he reveals the source of this joy: "For to me to live is Christ, and to die is gain" (1:21) and "I count everything as loss because of the surpassing worth of knowing Christ Jesus my Lord" (3:8) and "the peace of God, which surpasses all understanding, will guard your hearts and your minds in Christ Jesus" (4:7).

You might as well accept right now that this joy, this peace, transcends all understanding. We are simply never going to be able to explain or fully understand how or why this happens. But that's not all we are unable to fully grasp about God. Think about

it: we were lost in sin, yet God sent His Son into the flesh to die on the cross and to receive the punishment we deserved. Without the cross, we would die in our sins and be lost forever. God has gone to great lengths to make us His own, and through the power of the Holy Spirit, He lives in us and through us. All that's left for us to do is to give thanks to the One who understands everything that is simply too big for us to comprehend.

While we can't understand it, we can certainly strive to keep things in perspective. Many of our problems are simply not as important as how we look at them. Think about it: is it really that big of a deal that your husband would rather watch a game on TV than spend time with you? Should that be a deal breaker? Why not choose to sit with him during the game? Or is it really so awful that my bottom half is bigger than my top half? After all, they do make clothes in different shapes that fit my different shapes. And if your house has that lived-in look that makes it a bit messier than you'd like, you might be the only one bothered by it.

Let me acknowledge here and now that there are indeed those problems that are much more significant than these. There are issues of abuse, job loss, health crises, and death, to name only a few. I do not know what it feels like to lose a spouse, and I cannot, even in my wildest dreams, imagine the pain of losing a child. But I know what it feels like to lose my parents to cancer, and I watched my boss suffer from ALS. Yes, these are significant. And if you are facing issues of true significance, remember that you need not carry these burdens alone.

I am reminded of the story about a woman who entered an elevator, her arms loaded with heavy packages. As the doors closed, she heard someone say, "Ma'am, you can set your packages down and let the elevator carry them for you." We remember those words from Jesus in Matthew 11:28: "Come to Me, all who labor and are heavy laden, and I will give you rest." This is not an empty promise, for it comes from the very Savior who fulfilled God's promise to save us from our sins. Is anything too heavy for Him to bear? Let go of your burdens and place them at the foot of the cross. He will give you peace. It's all about perspective. Shalom!

Sane

Prayer: Dearest Lord Jesus, so often we join those who surrounded David, asking, "Who can show me some good?" Forgive us for such shallowness. Look upon us with favor, and grant us Your peace. **Amen.**

Sane

thursday

Personal Study Questions
Psalm 4:6–7

1. When have you heard someone ask, "Who will show us some good?" When have you personally wondered about how God could possibly keep His good promises in a distressing situation?

2. How does the light of God's face (v. 6b) answer the question posed earlier in the verse, answer even before the distressing circumstances are relieved?

3. Today's faith narrative tells us that peace is really all about perspective. Do you agree? How could that insight help you as you look at difficulties today through the lens of the cross?

4. When have you experienced the blessing of joy described in verse 7? How will you thank your Father for that joy?

Psalm 4:8

In peace I will both lie down and sleep;
*for You alone, O L*ORD*, make me dwell in safety.*

Don't Let the Bedbugs Bite

"Good night, sleep tight, don't let the bedbugs bite!" That's what Mom would say after prayers and good-night kisses as she tucked me into bed. As the five of us kids grew older, we'd say it in a chorus as our heads hit our pillows. It made me feel safe and secure. (I never let myself think about what a bedbug might do if it bit me; lions under my bed, however, were another matter!) This ritual ranks right up there as a favorite childhood memory, right next to the one of me falling asleep in

Sane

the backseat of the car just so my dad would have to carry me inside. Again, it made me feel safe and secure. And feeling safe and secure is—to borrow a popular word—priceless!

In this last verse of Psalm 4, David is able to rest his head in peace. Even in the midst of trouble, his anxieties are gone, and he feels safe and secure. What a perfect note to end on; what an incredible expression of David's faith. Although he had been consumed by calamities and brought to the point of utter distress, he did not sink under his sorrows, nor was he so broken that he stopped looking to God as his deliverer.

I am writing this on a Sunday afternoon. This morning, I went to church and sang in the choir. Somehow, the experience of blending voices in praise to God also brings a sense of safety and security—but I digress. At one point, a fellow soprano was led to search for a hymn her grandmother had chosen years earlier for her funeral. My friend found it in the section of the hymnal for Hope and Comfort. It's title? "Be Still, My Soul" (*LSB* 752), and it is based on Psalm 42.

I turned to it and found myself drawn in as I read the words and imagined the melody. The first stanza reads:

> *Be still, my soul; the Lord is on your side;*
> *Bear patiently the cross of grief or pain;*
> *Leave to your God to order and provide;*
> *In ev'ry change He faithful will remain.*
> *Be still, my soul; your best, your heav'nly Friend*
> *Through thorny ways leads to a joyful end.*

Isn't that precisely what David did? Didn't he leave it to God "to order and provide"?

Stanza 2 reads:

> *Be still, my soul; your God will undertake*
> *To guide the future as He has the past.*

Sane

Your hope, your confidence let nothing shake;
All now mysterious shall be bright at last.
Be still, my soul; the waves and winds still know
His voice who ruled them while He dwelt below.

Isn't that the same confidence David found—that God will guide the future just as He has the past?

In preparing to write this narrative, I turned to Psalm 42 and discovered that it is a prayer for restoration. Two verses in particular caught my attention: "Why are you cast down, O my soul, and why are you in turmoil within me? Hope in God; for I shall again praise Him, my salvation" (v. 5). "By day the LORD commands His steadfast love, and at night His song is with me, a prayer to the God of my life" (v. 8).

The problem with these so-called solutions is that they lead us into thinking that we can do something to bring peace to our hearts. But we can have only temporary and partial success at this because it's not we who bring the peace—it's God who brings the peace.

I can't help but wonder what song I carry with me as I lay my head on the pillow each night. Too often, it's a litany of the day's problems drumming a steady beat in my head. Or it's a refrain of the worries and anxieties I'm blowing way out of proportion. What if my lullaby became a litany of thanksgiving for the blessings that outweigh the problems? What if it were a recitation of Bible verses reminding me of God's great gifts of mercy, grace, and love?

Is something keeping you awake at night? Are you consumed with worry and anxiety? It's been said that worry is like a rocking chair; it gives you something to do, but it doesn't get you anywhere. We live in a frantic, fast-paced, information-overloaded society. I wouldn't be surprised to discover that most visits to the doctor are because of symptoms related to stress (as has been the case for me on more than one occasion). If you struggle with worry and anxiety, know that you are not alone.

Are you worried about your marriage or your kids? Do you fret about your job or who you should date? Are you concerned

Sane

that you can't make ends meet, or do you wonder how to pay for a current health crisis? Or are you simply obsessing about "what ifs"?

If so, you are robbing yourself of peace, and your worries are stealing your joy. If you are in crisis, first get the facts; then you will know "what is" rather than letting "what if" rule your thoughts. Then pray, giving your concerns and worries over to God, who loves you more than you will ever know. In Jeremiah 33:2–3, we read: "Thus says the Lord who made the earth, the Lord who formed it to establish it—the Lord is His name: Call to Me and I will answer you, and will tell you great and hidden things that you have not known."

In these words we find assurance that God will hear our prayers and answer them. The answer may not be what we asked for, and it may not come according to our timing, but we can be certain that God will act on our behalf and do what is best for us. And although the circumstances may not change on the outside, you will be different on the inside. The mayhem and chaos of worry and anxiety will have been brought into an order and focus that registers as peace.

Will the worries and anxieties return? Most certainly; after all, we live in a sinful world, and Satan is very familiar with our weaknesses and vulnerabilities. He latches onto them and reintroduces them whenever he can. They might be the same ones over and over, or he might introduce a new theme. Nonetheless, each time the worries come, we risk yet another onslaught on our bodies, our hearts, and our minds.

Several years ago, I read a column in our local newspaper on New Year's Day. As you might guess, it was about resolutions. The columnist wrote that she dealt with negative emotions by imagining herself standing in front of one of those revolving doors you see in a hotel or department store. She would visualize the emotion and then push it right out the revolving door. It might stay gone, or it might return (as if it had gotten stuck in the revolving door), but if it did return, she'd simply push it out again.

I've also seen worry dolls, especially when traveling in

Sane

Central America. These are small, very colorful dolls that come in a box. At night, you are supposed to tell your worries to the dolls and, as you place them in the box, you are to visualize shutting your worries away at the same time.

The problem with each of these so-called solutions is that they lead us into thinking that we can do something to bring peace to our hearts. But we can have only temporary and partial success at this because it's not we who bring the peace—it's God who brings the peace. Just as our salvation is not earned but is a gift of grace through the death and resurrection of Jesus Christ, so also is peace a gift of that grace. It can be ours only because Christ came to seek and to save the lost. We don't find Christ; He finds us. By the same token, we don't find peace; it finds us when our burdens are placed in the shadow of the cross.

We are made, loved, and cared for by a God who neither slumbers nor sleeps (Psalm 121:3). Along with David, we can feel safe and secure and find our rest in God, who made us, redeemed us, and keeps us in the one true faith.

So, good night, sleep tight. And don't let the bedbugs bite!

Prayer: Abba Father, help me to find peace and rest in the comfort of Your embrace, knowing that You will never, ever let me go! In the name and for the sake of Your Son, Jesus Christ, I pray. Amen.

Sane

Personal Study Questions
Psalm 4:8

1. What makes the words of "Be Still My Soul" (*LSB* 752), quoted in today's faith narrative, an appropriate summary of Psalm 4?

The Lord sustained me; God

2. Compare Psalm 4:8 with Psalm 3:5 and Psalm 127:2. What do all the verses tell us about God's gift of peace, even in times of grief and trouble?

3. When do you have trouble sleeping? How might these verses and the promises they contain help you then?

4. Only in the Lord do we enjoy true safety! What evidence of this can you cite from your own life?

Sane

Group Bible Study for Week 2
Psalm 4

1. What new insights or particularly encouraging thoughts did the Holy Spirit bring to your mind and heart as you explored Psalm 4 in the Scripture and through the words of the five faith narratives for this week?

2. Verse 1 includes a "then" and a "now" that follows from it. David first notes, "You have given me relief when I was in distress." He follows this statement describing past relief with a statement of his need now: "Be gracious to me and hear my prayer!" Tell about a time when remembering God's grace in the past gave you the courage you needed to approach God with a challenge in the present.

3. God hears when His children pray! Many of us have heard this truth since childhood and have come to take it for granted. Nevertheless, the fact is astonishing. David seems to pinch himself awake with astonishment in Psalm 3:4—"*He* answered *me!*"

   a. Where in Psalm 4 does David recall this same astonishing truth?

   b. When have you taken your Savior's listening ear for granted?

   c. In what ways do you find your Lord's willingness to hear and answer your prayers astonishing?

4. Situations that evoke feelings of distress and words of lamentation often evoke feelings of anger and agitation as well (v. 4). When have you experienced that?

5. How does David suggest we manage our anger and agitation (vv. 4–5)? (See also Psalm 51:17.) How might you personally and specifically act on the wisdom David shares here? What will you say to your Lord about that?

6. The faith narrative for Friday suggests this approach to worry: "If you are in crisis, first get the facts, for only then you will know 'what is' rather than letting 'what if' rule your thoughts. And then pray, giving your concerns and worries over to God, who loves you more than you will ever know." In what ways could this suggestion help you overcome the worries that often accompany life's crises?

7. How does verse 8 summarize and fittingly conclude this psalm?

Week Three

Psalm 5

[1] Give ear to my words, O Lᴏʀᴅ;
consider my groaning.

[2] Give attention to the sound of my cry,
my King and my God,
for to You do I pray.

[3] O Lᴏʀᴅ, in the morning You hear my voice;
in the morning I prepare a sacrifice for You and watch.

[4] For You are not a God who delights in wickedness;
evil may not dwell with You.

[5] The boastful shall not stand before Your eyes;
You hate all evildoers.

[6] You destroy those who speak lies;
the Lᴏʀᴅ abhors the bloodthirsty and deceitful man.

[7] But I, through the abundance of Your steadfast love,
will enter Your house.
I will bow down toward Your holy temple
in the fear of You.

[8] Lead me, O Lord, in Your righteousness
because of my enemies;
make Your way straight before me.

[9] For there is no truth in their mouth;
their inmost self is destruction;
their throat is an open grave;
they flatter with their tongue.

[10] Make them bear their guilt, O God;
let them fall by their own counsels;
because of the abundance of their transgressions cast them out,
for they have rebelled against You.

[11] But let all who take refuge in You rejoice;
let them ever sing for joy,
and spread Your protection over them,
that those who love Your name may exult in You.

[12] For You bless the righteous, O Lord;
You cover him with favor as with a shield.

Carla Fast

Psalm 5:1–3

Give ear to my words, O Lord; consider my groaning. Give attention to the sound of my cry, my King and my God, for to You do I pray. O Lord, in the morning You hear my voice; in the morning I prepare a sacrifice for You and watch.

The Best Part of the Day

A college friend once remarked that morning was her favorite part of the day. I happily agreed with her. She went on to describe the opening scene of the movie "The Sound of Music" when Maria enjoys a sunrise in the Austrian Alps. My friend, Linda, then began singing in her lovely alto

voice, "The hills are alive with the sound of music. . . . " Just then, she broke into the most awful screeching I have ever heard. After we laughed at her rendition, she explained that everything was not so great for Maria. The beauty of the scenery and the peace of the morning belied the terror of war that would soon affect her world.

Many years have passed since Linda butchered Maria's song. I still love mornings and think they are the best time of the day (my husband and son think I'm nuts!). For me, mornings are when everything is peaceful, when all is right with the world . . . well, not really, but I can pretend for a few moments before the day starts crowding in.

Consider the beginning of Psalm 5. David begins his morning with prayer. Apparently, prayer was David's usual way to begin his day, and this certainly is a nice way to start one's morning. After all, David had a lot on his mind. He had a kingdom to run, a family to take care of, and problems to settle with his neighbors. Sound familiar? It does to me. I have my kingdom to run (laundry never ends!), a family to see to, and everything that goes on inside and outside the house. It's overwhelming at times. Actually, it's more overwhelming than I'd like to admit. There are more than enough times when I can't handle everything, when I cry out for help, or when I just shut down and do nothing.

When I think I'm all alone at such times, I'm struck by the similarities between David's situation and mine. Look closely at how he describes prayer—"words," "groaning," "cry," "voice," a mixture of thoughts that fill his mind as he begins another day in his life as the king of Israel. Daily I stagger under the weight of my God-given responsibilities, my vocations. I know that as I do, the issues will continue as long as I am here.

Still, there's that moment in the morning when I first awaken, before reality sets in. You know that feeling? Peace. Contentment. But something starts nibbling at your conscience; something's wrong, but you're not sure what it is. Then, *bang*! It hits you head-on. You begin to recall the troubles from the previous day. Everything comes flooding back, and the peace you had

Carla

turns into a teasing whisper. You groan and bury your face in your pillow. Rise and shine! Time to start your day!

"Give ear to my words, O LORD; consider my groaning." David groaned. He cried. No doubt he often felt like rolling over and putting off the inevitable, but he knew that wasn't the solution. He knew that the answer to his prayers would not be found within himself but with God.

How could David be so sure? How can *anyone* be sure for that matter? There are times when I awaken and the new day is just like the day before. Nothing seems to change; God seems to be silent. I cry out to Him. "The sacrifices of God are a broken spirit; a broken and contrite heart, O God, You will not despise" (Psalm 51:17). David prepared a sacrifice—in repentance, he sacrificed the conviction of his old Adam, that the world rested on his shoulders. Prayer is the sweet-smelling aroma of such a sacrifice. The fact that David began with prayer showed his recognition that the day did not belong to him—it belongs to the Lord. David commended himself and his entire day to the Lord. Yet, in the midst of his prayer, he lamented. But David did not awaken and begin grumbling to his wife about the bills that were piling up or the troubles the kids were having in school. David took his problems to the One who can and will do something about them. "O LORD, be gracious to us; we wait for You. Be our arm every morning, our salvation in the time of trouble" (Isaiah 33:2).

It's amazing when you think about it. Each morning (or any time), we have special privileges because we have Daddy's ear. Through our Baptism, we became His daughters. Now we can climb into His lap and tell Him our troubles. He listens and helps. He promises to care for us.

How could David be so sure? How could he pray and watch? David could boldly approach God's throne of grace because he had special access to God. This access wasn't given to him because David was Israel's king or because he was such a good man. David was a sinner, deserving death and damnation—just like us. Yet he confidently approached God each and every morning. He approached his Father with all of the rights a child has to his parent's ear. David knew that God is a God of grace; David trusted

Carla

84

in the coming Messiah. By His sacrificial death and glorious resurrection, Jesus, David's hope and ours, brought us back into the good graces of our heavenly Father. His victory over death restored us and made us children of God. So David poured out his heart each morning to his Father—our Father, who loves us and cares for us and wants only good things for us. David dumped all of his troubles into the Lord's lap, knowing that God has a lap big enough to handle them. And what happened after he handed over all these troubles to the Lord? David watched and waited. He knew that the Lord blesses His children even through times of trouble.

So what about you and me? Like David, we have a wonderful gift: we can begin each day by spending time with our heavenly Father. It's amazing when you think about it. Each morning (or any time), we have special privileges because we have Daddy's ear. Through our Baptism into Christ (Romans 6:3–4), we became His daughters. Now we can climb into His lap and tell Him our troubles. He listens and helps. He promises to care for us. Do you remember when you were a little girl and you went to Mom or Dad with your problems? Remember the feeling of relief when they assured you that everything would be all right? The pressure was off. You could go about your day carefree and happy because your parents took your troubles away. It's still that way with God and you, Father and daughter.

So like David, we rise, we pray, we watch—and we confidently go about our day, expecting and receiving blessings from our heavenly Father. "The steadfast love of the LORD never ceases; His mercies never come to an end; they are new every morning; great is Your faithfulness" (Lamentations 3:22–23).

You know, when all was said and done, Linda was partially right. Things appear nice on the surface. The day breaks in a glorious sunrise with all the beauty it encompasses. Then, along with the day come dark clouds—troubles, sorrows, anxieties, despair. But when Linda stopped there, she failed to see the solution to these problems: the Morning Star that rises each day to take our problems on Himself. As we begin our day, we look to Christ our

Carla

Lord. We give Him all of our troubles, knowing that He works only good for His children in His perfect way and time. And in the meantime? We watch and wait and greet the day with confidence. After all, the day belongs to God . . . and so do we!

Prayer: Heavenly Father, thank You for making me Your child through the Word and water of Holy Baptism, and for giving me the privilege of calling upon You during the morning, evening, and any time of the day or night. Help me remember that all of my times are in Your loving hands and that You will always work good for me. In Jesus' name I pray. Amen.

Carla

monday

Personal Study Questions
Psalm 5:1–3

1. Like both Psalms 3 and 4, Psalm 5 expresses the psalmist's deep distress, especially as he considers seemingly countless enemies whose words and actions trouble him. In Psalm 5, David focuses his complaint on unbelievers, especially false teachers. Read Psalm 5 in its entirety.

   a. What words and phrases indicate that this psalm fits with other psalms of lament?

   b. In what ways have the words or actions of those who do not know and love Jesus caused you the kind of stress David expresses?

2. Consider the various words the writer uses to describe his prayers ("words," "groaning," and "cry"). Every morning, David's Savior-King hears his voice (v. 3). Consider also that your Savior "offered up prayers and supplications, with loud cries and tears, to Him who was able to save Him from death, and He was heard because of His reverence" (Hebrews 5:7).

   a. What prayers were on your heart as you awoke this morning?

   b. Recall times when your own prayers have taken the form of matter-of-fact words. When have your prayers become simply groans of frustration or pain? When have tears punctuated your prayers?

   c. How does it comfort you to know that Jesus understands how it feels to pray when tears and groans replace words? What will you say to Him right now?

Carla

Psalm 5:4–6

For You are not a God who delights in wickedness;
evil may not dwell with You. The boastful shall
not stand before Your eyes; You hate all evildoers.
You destroy those who speak lies; the LORD
abhors the bloodthirsty and deceitful man.

Dreams Become Realities

Have you ever realized while dreaming that you were dreaming? Having such a realization can be convenient if the dream is a nightmare. You can actually tell yourself that what is happening isn't real so there's no need to worry. (Okay, this doesn't always work!) Have you had the opposite experience, when you wished you *were* dreaming because the reality was too hard to bear? This happens to people more than we realize. Behind the smiles and laughter, there can

Carla

be a great deal of pain.

As I write this, my son is being systematically bullied at his school. It's a nightmare—but we're all awake. And while I'm upset about it, my son is the one who is living it. In the middle of our nightmare comes Psalm 5:4–6. The words of the psalmist about evildoers who sin repeatedly and without remorse pound in my head. If ever there was an example of true evildoers, it's the students who continually harass my son verbally and physically. The mother in me wants to race to school, yank those kids out of class, and throttle them. I'm filled with such righteous anger at these kids who are picking on my child. It's so frustrating that I want to scream—and sometimes I do. But usually I cry and pray—aloud, silently, in the car, at home, at the fast-food joint. And I put on a brave face to help my son with the heavy load he bears each day.

David speaks of God's hatred of evildoers, of His abhorrence of those who boast or lie or deceive. I've always imagined that these people compose some sort of special club. They meet in a dark hovel in the most desolate area in town to plot their next attack. Actually, this might have been true in David's case. He did have a lot of enemies planning attacks upon him, enemies from within and without, of all sizes and shapes. Think of Goliath the Philistine. What a braggart! His size alone made him stand out, but combined with his arrogance and his taunts of David and the Israelites, Goliath was quite a bold, in-your-face bully.

Now, had I been David, I would have quaked in my sandals, cried, and then turned and run. But David didn't. Why? Because he was young? No. Because he was brave? No. Because he was strong? Not likely. There was nothing in that shepherd boy to suggest that he could defeat this evil giant. David knew it. And Goliath knew it too. But David went to fight because it was God's fight. God, the God of the Israelites, would take on this bully and destroy him and all he stood for. He was unfit to stand in God's presence, and he would no longer be allowed to boast.

But what about the evil giants in our lives? Our Lord taught us to pray, "Lead us not into temptation, but deliver us from evil." Society's conception of evil varies. Some see evil as a movie char-

Carla

acter with a grotesque face and snarling lips; others deny that evil even exists. But you and I already have discovered, perhaps many times over, that evil comes in all sizes and shapes and ways. Consider the evildoers in our world: the co-worker who stabs us in the back; the neighbors who have their own definition of the word *neighborly*; society in general, which seems bent on eradicating all the morals and values we so earnestly try to instill in our families. All of these bullies seem to have us first on their agendas. Back to the original question—what can we do? Herein lies the problem: *we* can't do anything. It is God who can, and will, take care of us—and them. "As the mountains surround Jerusalem, so the LORD surrounds His people, from this time forth and forevermore" (Psalm 125:2). God promises to care for us, His children, throughout our lives. David understood this and prayed to God in confidence that He would hear his cry and would not abandon him. How comforting it is to know we can do the same! As God's children, we have our Father's ear, and our pleading for protection does not go unheeded.

> *The blessed exchange, Jesus' taking our sins upon Himself and giving us His righteousness, was the Father's plan of salvation. It was the greatest act of love for humankind— for us, and even for the evildoers who plague us.*

Of course, there's always a part of me (sinful me, doubting me, old Adam me) that says, "Okay, so why don't things get better? Shouldn't we live in peace and quiet since we're the people of God?" Hardly. Consider Jesus' time on earth and His warning that the world would hate us because of Him. But consider something else—in all fairness, we should be grouped with the bad guys of this world. Sad, but true. We may get a little testy when we're reminded of this. After all, we haven't done such things as they have; we haven't beaten anybody; we haven't planned another's downfall. In fact, when our actions are compared with theirs side by side, we end up looking pretty nice. But look more closely. God always looks closely. He sees our sin. He knows our hearts are just as corrupt as the bully's down the street. As Psalm 5 declares, God knows the evildoers and will destroy them. Does that give us pause? It should, because evil is no

Carla

joke. It can't be brushed aside. It certainly is not to be trifled with. Evil is a part of us. It surrounds us, and it will lead to our eternal destruction—unless Someone steps in to save us. And that's just what God did. Our righteous and holy Father set about to destroy sin once and for all so we could be free of its everlasting condemnation, its evil ways, and its hold on us.

God did not spare His own Son, "but gave Him up for us all" (Romans 8:32). Perhaps we can get a peek at just how damning sin is and what the only way to destroy it is when we look at the unfolding of God's promise to save us from evil. Sin must be paid for, and the only One who could pay the price was God the Son. So great is the Father's love for us that He set about the death of Jesus to make this payment on our behalf. When Christ was on earth, He suffered at the hands of the vilest bullies, those who would stop at nothing to hurt Him. He willingly allowed Himself to be tortured and crucified because He was doing His Father's will. And where was God the Father during all of this? He was leading the pack!

What?

That's exactly what He did. The blessed exchange, Jesus' taking our sins upon Himself and giving us His righteousness, was the Father's plan of salvation. It was the greatest act of love for humankind—for us, and even for the evildoers who plague us. Christ died for them as well. If they remain in sin, they get what they deserve. They will be destroyed and eternally damned. Their brief moment of triumph on earth is a false victory flag waving in a wind that will change direction in eternity.

We, on the other hand, get what we *don't* deserve—forgiveness, life, salvation. Through Baptism, all the benefits of the cross—the crucifixion and the resurrection of Jesus Christ—are delivered to us. Instead of fleeing because we know God is angry with us and out to destroy us, we run to our Father in confident anticipation. Because of Christ, our sins are no longer counted against us. We are once more His beloved children, saved and protected from all that would harm us—including bullies, including ourselves.

Carla

It comes down to this: when I cry out to God at the injustice of evildoers; when I weep at the harm I do to others; when the mother bear in me wants to claw at those hurting my cub, I call on the Lord for forgiveness and strength. Just as the proper authorities are dealing with my son's case, so David reminds me that God is the final authority in all things. He will deal with all evildoers and protect His children. Paul believed it and wrote, "For I am sure that neither death nor life, nor angels nor rulers, nor things present nor things to come, nor powers, nor height nor depth, nor anything else in all creation, will be able to separate us from the love of God in Christ Jesus our Lord" (Romans 8:38–39). God hears our laments and holds us in His loving arms. We, like David, pray to Him, confident that He does. He will see us safely through our nightmares, real and otherwise, and take us to our home with Him in heaven—a dream come true!

Prayer: Dearest Lord, evil impacts everything from my work to my family. Help me to rely upon Your strength and promise to be with me. Comfort me with Your presence and Your promise of protection and deliverance. Use the times of trial to bring me closer to You, for You alone are my life and my salvation. In Jesus' name and for His sake I pray. **Amen.**

Carla

tuesday

Personal Study Questions
Psalm 5:4–6

1. Today's reading from Psalm 5 introduces the reasons behind the psalmist's groans and cries—the wicked, evil, boastful, bloodthirsty, and deceitful people all around him. "Evildoers" (v. 5) are those who break God's Law repeatedly and refuse to let Him bring them to repentance and faith.

   a. Why do you suppose this causes the psalmist such anguish? Why can't he just "live and let live"?

   b. Have the words and actions of evildoers ever caused you anguish similar to that described in today's faith narrative? similar to that in verses 4–6? Explain.

2. Verse 4 makes a strong point by using this understatement: "You are not a God who delights in wickedness."

   a. What does this sentence mean? What is God's attitude toward wickedness?

   b. If "evil may not dwell with [God]" (v. 4), how does the psalmist expect to do so? How do you?

Carla

Psalm 5:7–8

But I, through the abundance
of Your steadfast love, will enter Your house.
I will bow down toward Your holy temple
in the fear of You. Lead me, O LORD, in Your righteousness
because of my enemies; make Your way straight before me.

Lead Me,
Keep Me

When I was in high school, a group of friends and I decided to wrap a house with toilet paper (some call it "TP-ing"). Now, we were essentially a nice group that affectionately decorated the yards of people we liked, and this excursion was no exception. There were about ten of us who headed out that evening, but we were soon joined by some party crashers.

At first, when the car drove by, we weren't that con-

Carla

94

cerned. We knew the neighborhood—we lived there. It was only eleven o'clock on a beautiful Friday night, and we were out for a stroll. What could go wrong? It was when the car approached the second time and slowed down that John, my next-door neighbor, softly said, "Uh-oh."

As I glanced in the direction he was staring, I saw the car stop. My heart jumped! Six of the biggest guys I had ever seen emerged from the vehicle. I remember wondering how they fit in the car; they were that huge. And not only that, they were older— mid-twenties by my estimate.

It didn't take long to see what was happening. Within seconds, they had surrounded us with a casualness that belied their intentions. By now we were in the middle of the road, and it seemed to me that the streetlights had gone out.

We did the only thing we could—we kept walking. But the men stayed with us and the tension kept building—until it was broken by my squeaky "Hi!" Wrong move. Immediately everyone stopped. Their leader stepped forward. "You got any women here?" he demanded. Ever the busybody, I started to reply, only to have John grab my hand and wrench it as hard as he could.

Taking advantage of my throbbing distraction, John took over. "Women? Huh! You've got to be kidding. I mean we have a couple of girls here, but they're pretty ugly. Nothing to interest any of you." Still being a bit naïve, I started to protest, but again John saved me from myself. He stomped on my foot!

After a long, long moment of silence and dread, the men sauntered back to their car and left. My friends and I stood there for a few moments, staring at one another. In an effort to alleviate the tension, John quipped, "You know, I was so afraid, I thought I was going to need to use this toilet paper!" As we laughed, we also acknowledged our relief at being freed from the evil that had enveloped us. Only later did I understand the seriousness of the situation—the enemies that surrounded us, their evil intentions, our helplessness to stop it or save ourselves. Truly God prevented these men from harming us that evening.

While our lives don't usually involve such physically dra-

Carla

matic episodes, they nevertheless include enemies that try to surround and close in upon us. No matter where you turn, something or someone is out to destroy you. The root of all these evils is sin. David knew sin—he experienced it time and again. He was a sinner himself; he was also a victim of sin. He was pounded by enemies of his kingdom and frequently found the enemy to be within himself. And he knew that these were not just ordinary foes; they were foes that were set out to separate him from God. So what did David do? He prayed repeatedly to the Lord to guide him, give him wisdom, lead him in the right direction, and make his path safe.

Over Satan's din, there is an even greater voice, louder than that of our enemy. It's God's voice—His loving call for you to make a U-turn, to repent and turn away from your sins. David heard this call and cried out to God, confident of His mercy.

Why would David pray this way? For the same reason we do—he knew he was a sinner, too weak to withstand the attacks on him. Look closely at verses 7 and 8. David prayed that God would lead him through the midst of his enemies, making his path straight. And where did that path lead? To the Lord's temple, to the Lord Himself, where David would find security and blessings in abundance. He knew that through the Messiah, we are made righteous, and we can approach our heavenly Father in confidence. And he trusted God to keep His promises.

Like David, we know that God certainly guides our steps. How many times have you had a near tragedy and thanked God for safely seeing you through it? Can you think of situations where a member of your family avoided a catastrophe and you thought, *Only by the grace of God did he or she come out safely?* We rejoice when we realize that He has rescued us again.

But what about the other times? The times when it seems that evil has the upper hand? The times when we're bombarded from all sides by enemies who would destroy us? You know the enemies I'm talking about. They are many—large and small, living, dead, or otherwise. One enemy might be gossip that has torn your family apart. Reputations once sullied are often impossible to repair. One enemy might be the cancer that has affected you

Carla

or a loved one. It not only eats away at the patient's health, but it can attack your faith as you struggle to understand why this disease occurred. Or perhaps you are assailed by the breakdown of a relationship. Has a divorce or estrangement wreaked havoc in your world or that of your children?

Then, too, when we're not bombarded by evils outside of us, there is always evil within. Our bodies turn against us as we struggle with physical, mental, and emotional illness. To make it worse, our sinful selves are hell-bent (literally) on making trouble. Our old Adam is alive and well. He certainly doesn't want to hear that not only do we deserve all of the evil that comes our way, but a lot of it is our own fault. "Against You, You only, have I sinned and done what is evil in Your sight" (Psalm 51:4). Many of the troubles from without and within are our just rewards, and at times, when we realize the enormity of our sin, it's enough to make us want to curl up and die. This is exactly what Satan wants. He is tickled when I despair at the enemies surrounding me. He laughs when I consider everything to be hopeless. And he dances with joy when I turn away from the Lord. I can even hear his words echoing to our mother, Eve: "Did God really say . . . ?" Did God really say, Eve, that He loves you? If He really loves you, wouldn't He keep all of this from happening to you?

And you too?

Over Satan's din, there is an even greater voice, louder than that of our enemy. It's God's voice—His loving call for you to make a U-turn, to repent and turn away from your sins. David heard this call and cried out to God, confident in His mercy. David prayed in Psalm 27:11, "Teach me Your way, O LORD, and lead me on a level path because of my enemies." This level path is one without obstacles, one that cannot deter us or keep us from Christ's salvation. It is the path Jesus Himself took before us, removing the stones of our enemies, making it smooth and straight so we could follow Him. And what was this path Jesus took? It was the Via Dolorosa, the way of sorrows. He took on our flesh and followed His Father's plan of rescue. Consider what He endured: taunts, jeers, lies, torture, crucifixion, and finally, estrangement

Carla

from God the Father, His Father. And yet, at the end of this road leading to death, Jesus emerged victorious. Arising from His tomb, He came out the winner, and because of Him, so do we. We are united with Him in our Baptism, and this means that no matter what kind of enemy surrounds us, we emerge as victors too. Our foes cannot stop us—even if they kill us. They have no permanent hold on us, for we belong to Christ. "You will not abandon my soul to Hades, or let Your Holy One see corruption. You have made known to me the paths of life; You will make me full of gladness with Your presence" (Acts 2:27–28).

So now, as you encounter enemies and times when you feel lost and alone, remember that the Gospel calls to you. God's way of repentance and faith will comfort you as you move forward, already gifted with His life and salvation. God's Word and Sacraments will strengthen and sustain you. Each step of the way, you can call upon the Lord for mercy and blessings and, like David, confidently pray that the Lord will keep you on His path and will not let you stumble along the way. You *will* reach the temple of the Lord, the heavenly home He has prepared for David and for you, for Jesus is the Way.

Prayer: Dear Father in heaven, You know my enemies surround me. You understand the troubles I face day in and day out. Don't let them keep me from coming into Your presence and receiving Your gifts. Lead me to repent of my sins, and comfort me with Your forgiveness and mercy. Keep me in Your path of righteousness, and hold me in Your loving arms as You lead me to my heavenly home with You. In Jesus' name I pray. Amen.

Carla

wednesday

Personal Study Questions
Psalm 5:7–8

1. Verse 7 begins with the word *but*. This word introduces a stark contrast—verses 4–6 and verses 7–8.

   a. Summarize this contrast.

   b. Isn't the psalmist being boastful or even arrogant? Why or why not?

2. Can you confidently enter God's house, bowing toward His holy temple just as the psalmist does? Explain.

3. The author of today's faith narrative writes, "Our foes cannot stop us—even if they kill us. They have no permanent hold on us, for we belong to Christ." Do you believe this? Why? How does it comfort you?

Carla

Psalm 5:9–10

For there is no truth in their mouth; their inmost self is destruction; their throat is an open grave; they flatter with their tongue. Make them bear their guilt, O God; let them fall by their own counsels; because of the abundance of their transgressions cast them out, for they have rebelled against You.

False Teachers

The mother of one of my dearest girlhood friends was a source of both inspiration and confusion for me. When I was young, I admired her greatly. She was my picture of the ideal lady—quiet, unassuming, graceful, witty. She was well educated and a lover of classical music. But there was so much more to her. She had a special connection to God. She was obviously favored by our Lord. How did I know? Because Fran, her daughter and my friend, told me, and her mother confirmed it. She would pray for rain and God would make it rain the next day. She would pray

Carla

for healing and God would grant her request. I was more than a little in awe of her.

Yet, something wasn't right. I couldn't quite put my finger on it, but I knew Fran and her mother were telling me things that went against what I knew from Scripture. Then they informed me that I did not have enough faith in God. At the time, I had the flu. Fran's mother said if my faith were strong enough, I would pray to God to heal me and He would. I said my illness had nothing to do with the strength of my faith; it was a virus of some sort. Obviously I had a way to go in the faith department. Fran smiled at me as an instructor would at an impertinent student, then changed the subject. I puzzled over this for a long time, but I didn't talk about it. That is, until I brought it up with my husband years later.

Fast forward. Fran and I now lived in different regions of the country, but we met at a reunion. After the formalities were out of the way, she launched into news of her mother. Since I had married a pastor, Fran thought that I must be okay in the faith department now and treated me as an equal. She explained how her mother had been infected with *e. coli* and had become gravely ill. Fran and her family prayed over her and reclaimed her mother's health in Jesus' name. Her mother did become better—after several weeks in the hospital, lots of medicine, and the service of competent doctors. I expressed my happiness at the news, but I didn't comment on the "name it and claim it" beliefs she still espoused. My thoughts were running along these lines: "What will you do when your mother actually dies? What exactly is your faith based on? And who is your god?" I no longer just had a hunch that something was wrong with this woman's beliefs. I now understood that she trusted more in the power of her faith than in the promises of her God. Ultimately, she was attempting to draw me away from the Gospel and from Christ Himself.

In today's portion of Psalm 5, we find David praying for God's justice against a special group of evildoers—false teachers. These people are particularly abhorrent because their words can have an eternal impact upon those who listen to them. Just look

Carla

at the words *false teacher*. Do you see the irony? A teacher is all about proclaiming truths to students. A false teacher deliberately sets out to deceive those under her tutelage.

Throughout history, including David's time, false teachers have abounded. David was rightly concerned about the liars who tried to discredit him and cause his kingdom to fall—those false teachers bent on destroying all who followed the true God. In verse 9, David rightly declares that these false teachers flattered with their tongues, but their mouths were open graves. With their words, they led others to death—physically and eternally. Yet, rather than seeking revenge, David called upon the Lord to address these enemies.

When the false teachers abound, when they say your faith isn't strong enough or you haven't done enough for Christ, even when your own conscience says you're not good enough for Him— agree with them! Then remember that it's not about you—it's about Jesus for you.

In our time, we also fight against liars and false teachers. Our world changes rapidly, but there's really nothing new. Like David, we are living during a time when Christianity is threatened and Christians are persecuted. Islam is claiming more followers while disciples of the true God—Father, Son, and Holy Spirit—seem to be fewer in number. But it's always been like that. False teachers entice people with their words, but these words are empty, lifeless.

Now, I know that a faithful Muslim imam does not preach or teach about the true Christ, who is both fully God and fully man. False teachings like that are obvious—and I avoid them. But it's the subtle false teachings that quickly surround me and draw me into their web. These are the lies that appear to be true until they are unwrapped to reveal their deception. As I write this, a movie is being made from a popular children's novel whose author has stated that the purpose of the book is to draw children away from Christ. There are other examples in the world: media output that derides Christian values and beliefs, the subtle encroachment of humanism upon society, even false teaching within the Church.

Are you surprised? Don't be. "Watch out for those who cause divisions and create obstacles contrary to the doctrine that you

Carla

have been taught; avoid them. For such persons do not serve our Lord Christ, but their own appetites, and by smooth talk and flattery they deceive the hearts of the naive" (Romans 16:17–18). David calls upon God to have these people bear their guilt and fall because of their sins. And they will, for false teachers pervert God's Word and His message of salvation found in Christ alone. God will deal with them. Still, in our world, they run rampant in ways that appeal to our sinful nature. From "Christian" novels in which the heroes make their commitments to the Lord to groups that say, "Sure, Jesus died on the cross for you, now all you have to do is your part (give your heart to Him, do your best)," false teachers are alive and well. Their message sounds good. It has a nice ring to it. It flatters my ego and my sense of righteousness—and my sinful self *loves* the idea of having a part in my salvation, even if it's just a little part.

But when I open a different book, and when I attend the Divine Service, I find something else altogether: "You were dead in the trespasses and sins" (Ephesians 2:1); "For by grace you have been saved through faith. And this is not your own doing; it is the gift of God, not a result of works, so that no one may boast" (Ephesians 2:8–9). So, dead sinner that I am, I'm unable on my own to make any decision to follow Jesus. But wait! There's still that commitment thing! Yes, but it's *God* who does the committing, who sent His Son to save us from our sins. So there you have it. Many Christians believe they have a helping hand in their salvation. In reality, however, God does it all.

So when the false teachers abound, when they say your faith isn't strong enough or you haven't done enough for Christ, even when your own conscience says you're not good enough for Him—agree with them! Then remember that it's not about you—it's about Jesus *for* you. God forgives you and restores you through His Son. He strengthens you through His Word and Sacraments, keeping you in the true faith, the faith of David, faith in the Messiah. David knew that in the end, the words of false teachers lead to death; but the Word made flesh brings forgiveness, life, and salvation.

Carla

Prayer: Lord Jesus, You and You alone are my Savior. Keep false teachers from distorting Your Word. Protect me from all that would keep me from You and Your salvation. When I stray, forgive me and bring me back to You, and keep me in my baptismal faith to the end. I ask in Your name. **Amen.**

Carla

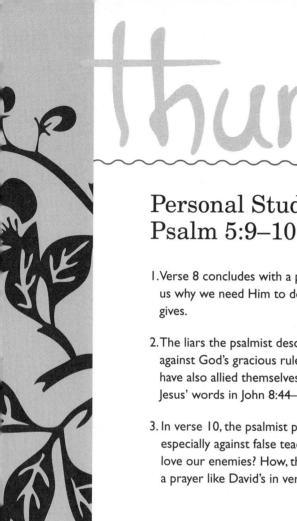

thursday

Personal Study Questions
Psalm 5:9–10

1. Verse 8 concludes with a plea that God lead us. Verse 9 tells us why we need Him to do so. Summarize the reasons David gives.

2. The liars the psalmist describes in verse 9 have rebelled against God's gracious rule. As if that weren't enough, they have also allied themselves with Satan. What insights do Jesus' words in John 8:44–45 add?

3. In verse 10, the psalmist prays for justice against the wicked, especially against false teachers. Doesn't Jesus teach us to love our enemies? How, then, can His inspired Word include a prayer like David's in verse 10?

Carla

Psalm 5:11–12

But let all who take refuge in You rejoice; let them ever sing for joy, and spread Your protection over them, that those who love Your name may exult in You. For You bless the righteous, O LORD; You cover him with favor as with a shield.

A Shield Strong to Save

It was a dark and stormy night. . . . No, really, it was! And someone was trying to break into our house. We were vulnerable and afraid: one woman and two teenage girls. My sister Lisa attempted to scare the prowler banging on our bedroom window, trying to get in. "Dad! There are burglars! Get the gun!" Did the bluff work? We didn't wait to find out. We arrived at Mom's room within moments, urgently telling her what had happened.

Our mother appeared calm as she walked into the kitchen, a frightened girl attached to each arm. Without

Carla

106

turning on the lights, she phoned the police. After explaining the situation, she hung up, then turned to face us. "They're on their way. Let's stay by the phone until they get here."

It seemed like hours, but in a few minutes there was a knock on the front door. After Mom asked who was there, she opened it to see a policeman, completely soaked, standing on the stoop. "Thank you for coming so quickly!" she breathed. "Did you see anyone?"

"Ma'am, my partner and I have already searched your property," he replied. "There's no one around. No footprints either. I think I know what happened, though. These winds are so strong that one of your storm shutters blew off the window, and it's lying in your front yard! Looks like the screws that held it in place weren't tightened enough." Mom gratefully thanked the officer and closed the door. After a few minutes, we decided we were too keyed up to sleep, so we got a snack and discussed the incident. The next day, Mom had that shutter repaired and the others checked for security.

Years later, this story is still a family favorite. Now we can laugh, but then we couldn't. While the danger wasn't real, our fear was. Our home proved to be less than adequate as a shield. The storm shutter, designed to protect against powerful winds, was literally blown away. And not only did we fear the elements that evening, we also feared the evil of man. We thought our home was a refuge, a shield against outside dangers. Instead, it became a trap from which we couldn't free ourselves. So we called the authorities, the ones whose job it was to rescue us—and they did just that.

In the final verses of Psalm 5, David speaks about God's saving work. Throughout this psalm, we have read how David was persecuted by his enemies. They were many and they were ruthless. David knew these encounters would never cease because those who live in this world will suffer from sin and its effects. David recognized that he needed protection; he knew he was unable to save himself from attack, but he was confident of his protector—the Lord Himself. And he prayed fervently, ceaselessly,

Carla

and confidently. Thus, David ends the psalm rejoicing in the fact that God blesses him and covers him as a shield, protecting him as he lived on earth.

What about you? Are you under attack? Do you feel enemy arrows and spears being fired in your direction? They can be just as relentless as those aimed at David. The world itself is your enemy. "If the world hates you, know that it has hated Me before it hated you" (John 15:18). How often do you have to remind yourself or your family that as Christians, you're countercultural? Your values and lifestyle might seem strange and archaic in a society that professes truth to be relative. And then those enemies reach into your home. Try as you might to make your house a safe haven, a refuge from the ills of the world, you still fail. You vow to leave your problems at work; you encourage your kids to associate with other Christian children; you limit the amount of television and other media to curb their influence on your family. And still you are hit with the arrows of the enemy.

When you encounter the enemies that want to destroy you, remember that the arms once opened to die for you are now open to shield you. Christ is your refuge. Call upon His name, for you, like David, are His redeemed, His own, His favorite.

If that's not enough, there's always you yourself! Is your body attacking you? Are you suffering from an illness or disease, mental or physical? I've been dealing with depression since my teens. Medication helps when it flares up, but the better help comes from my husband. He holds and comforts me, acting as my protector. The best thing he does, however, is to point me to Someone stronger—Someone who is truly stronger than my attacker.

Illnesses plague us, never letting us forget that we are sinners who will one day die. We suffer attacks upon our bodies and cry out in frustration. How sad it is, therefore, to also realize that often we are the attackers throwing arrows at others. Our motives, if we're honest, are far from innocent. In my case, it's really quite simple: I want everything to go my way. I know what's best for me and everyone else. So, from trying to run people's lives to letting my words get away from me, I proceed to make a mess of

Carla

things. "For I have the desire to do what is right, but not the ability to carry it out. For I do not do the good I want, but the evil I do not want is what I keep on doing" (Romans 7:18b–19). It boils down to my problem with the First Commandment. Basically, I want to be God. My sinful nature wants to control everything and everyone as I try to make a little heaven here on earth. Instead of harmony and contentment, however, I find myself frustrated with my life, my home, my self, still failing to acknowledge that I'm the enemy in this instance.

At some point, when you feel bombarded from all sides, when you have nowhere to turn for help, you might want to scream. (I have, but other than scaring a flock of ducks, it didn't really do anything!) You will finally realize that you're not able to cope with these attacks, these enemies, and if help is going to be had, it has to come from outside of you. But Satan is there, ready to tell you that it's pointless . . . there is no help . . . you might as well give up. Then, as you open your mouth to cry "Uncle!' say "Father!" instead. Call upon the name of the Lord, as David did. Pray confidently and fervently, for God, our heavenly Father, is the authority—the One whose job it is to rescue us—and He will not fail. God hears us and will shield us, covering us with His favor.

But why would God do this? Certainly not because of any good we have done. David, while being a great king, had a lot of problems. He was an adulterer, a murderer, a bigamist, a king with enemies all around. He had a lot in common with us—sin, the need for a Savior, and the inability to save himself. Back to the question—why would God help us? Because of His great love for us. He sent His Son to rescue us when we were unable to save ourselves. Jesus came to earth where He was taunted, beaten, and sacrificed for all for us—in our place. Our living Shield absorbed all the shots aimed at us so we could receive forgiveness, life, and salvation. He took our deadly attacks and gave us life in return. And by His sacrifice, Jesus won God's favor for us. Now we are the "favor-ites" of God—those whom His favor covers as a shield, for "If God is for us, who can be against us?" (Romans 8:31b).

So you and I continue in our world, in our daily tasks, in

Carla

109

the midst of attack from all sides. At times, you may feel the arrows whizzing by; at others, you may experience pain as they hit their targets and cause you to crumple under their might. Still, in the midst of such sufferings, remember that your battles here on earth will eventually end. When they do, you will enjoy victory in its fullness, for by His death and resurrection, Jesus has already won the victory for you. Until then, when you encounter the enemies that want to destroy you, remember that the arms once opened to die for you are now open to shield you. Christ is your refuge. Call upon His name, for you, like David, are His redeemed, His own, His favorite.

You shall seek those who contend with you, but you shall not find them; those who war against you shall be as nothing at all. For I, the LORD your God, hold your right hand; it is I who say to you, "Fear not, I am the one who helps you" . . . declares the LORD; your Redeemer is the Holy One of Israel. Isaiah 41:12–14

Prayer: Lord Jesus, You suffered, died, and rose again to defeat my enemies. Your gifts of forgiveness, life, and salvation are the spoils of war You won for me. Be my shield, for You alone are my protection and refuge. Keep me safe in Your arms until You bring me to my heavenly home. I ask in Your name. *Amen.*

Carla

Friday

Personal Study Questions
Psalm 5:11–12

1. Today's faith narrative describes a time in the author's life when her fear was real although the danger was not. When have you experienced something similar?

2. Verse 11 begins with "but" and another contrast. How would you describe it?

3. When have you most recently rejoiced in God's refuge, in His protecting presence?

4. Compare Psalm 3:3 with 5:12. Why might we want to visualize this shield as bearing the sign of the cross?

Carla

Group Bible Study for Week 3
Psalm 5

1. Which faith narrative for the week did you find most helpful or meaningful as you explored an admittedly difficult psalm? Explain.

2. While Psalm 5 falls under the "Psalms of Lament" category, it also has some characteristics of the "Imprecatory Psalms." Imprecatory psalms implore God to judge the wicked.

    a. What does the psalmist lament in verses 4–6 and 9–10?

    b. Could you comfortably pray this psalm, and verse 10 in particular? Why or why not?

    c. When and how do you pray for Christ's enemies, especially those who teach falsehoods and lead others astray? Based on what you've seen as you've studied Psalm 5, how might you change your practice?

3. Psalm 5 begins with words similar to those that begin Psalm 4. What similarities do you see? What inspires the psalmist's confident approach to a holy God?

4. How might you pray the words of this psalm as you face a different kind of enemy? For example, to which verses or passages might you turn if you were anguishing over health challenges? financial concerns? gossip? a son or daughter, grandson or granddaughter, who had fallen from faith? Explain.

5. Verse 12 promises that our God covers us with His favor "as with a shield."

a. What do you understand that to mean?

b. Tell about a time when knowing that would help you "speak the truth in love" (Ephesians 4:15) to one of the false teachers described in verse 9.

Week Four

Psalm 6

[1] O Lord, rebuke me not in Your anger,
nor discipline me in Your wrath.

[2] Be gracious to me, O Lord, for I am languishing;
heal me, O Lord, for my bones are troubled.

[3] My soul also is greatly troubled.
But You, O Lord—how long?

[4] Turn, O Lord, deliver my life;
save me for the sake of Your steadfast love.

[5] For in death there is no remembrance of You;
in Sheol who will give You praise?

[6] I am weary with my moaning;
every night I flood my bed with tears;
I drench my couch with my weeping.

[7] My eye wastes away because of grief;
it grows weak because of all my foes.

[8] Depart from me, all you workers of evil,
for the Lord has heard the sound of my weeping.

[9] The Lord has heard my plea;
the Lord accepts my prayer.

[10] All my enemies shall be ashamed and greatly troubled;
they shall turn back and be put to shame in a moment.

Rose E. Adle

Psalm 6:1–3

O LORD, rebuke me not in Your anger, nor discipline me in Your wrath. Be gracious to me, O LORD, for I am languishing; heal me, O LORD, for my bones are troubled. My soul also is greatly troubled. But You, O LORD—how long?

How Long?

ne Saturday afternoon, my parents announced that they'd rented a movie for us to watch together called *The Neverending Story*. Movies were a special treat in our family, and we all oohed and aahed with excitement. First, though, my mom and dad had to get some work done, so

we were instructed to go play until they called us. Hide-and-seek was the game *du jour*.

One of my little brothers (the smallest of us) hid behind a set of metal shelves in our basement where the nonperishable food items were stacked. We didn't find him, but eventually, we heard him. Better put, we heard the crash. Sensing that we'd given up our search, he untucked himself from his nook behind the shelving unit, and the whole thing fell to the floor. I surveyed the surreal scene from the top of the steps. Dented cans rolled this way and that across the smooth concrete. Contents of countless broken jars oozed together in the mess to end all messes. And there was my brother, standing in the midst of the muddle, with the look of someone who knew he was a dead man.

Dad raced down the stairs, scooped him up, hugged him, and asked if he was hurt. He checked for cuts and bruises. Seeing none, he carried my brother across the grotesque river of applesauce, pickles, spaghetti sauce, and maple syrup so he'd not be harmed by the shards of glass. Once upstairs, my dad put a firm hand on the shoulder of his ill-behaved son and escorted him to a corner in the kitchen. Tears streamed down the little face. Clearly heartbroken, he looked up at our father and, through choked sobs, he asked, "How long?"

The question he asked that day is one we've all posed. The agony that is so real in this world drives us to the same place. Surrounded by suffering and its very real effects, we can't help but ask when it will be over.

How long?

The writer of Psalm 6 is himself no stranger to this desperate cry. He writes in the first three verses: "O Lord, rebuke me not in Your anger, nor discipline me in Your wrath. Be gracious to me, O Lord, for I am languishing; heal me, O Lord, for my bones are troubled. My soul also is greatly troubled. But You, O Lord—how long?" The psalmist is pained in both body and soul, and, like any human, he wants it to cease.

We bring the world down around us by our own rebellious ways. Although it is sometimes unintentional (like my brother's

Rose

carelessness), we sin, and we suffer for it. When a teenager is grounded for breaking curfew, she asks, "How long?" How long until she can reclaim her social life? After screaming at her husband in a burst of unwarranted hysteria, a wife asks, "How long?" How long will he be angry with her?

Chastisement seems to drag on and on, even if we know it's for our own good. Hebrews 12:6 says that the Lord disciplines the one He loves and chastises every son He receives. That doesn't make it feel any better though. The pain in this world is so deep that we fear it will go on forever. My little brother probably thought his punishment was as interminable as the title of the movie we were watching in the other room. When it is our fault, we cry out in agony, but at least our innate sense of fairness makes it more bearable.

Life's a mess, but when we stand hopelessly and helplessly in the midst of tragedy, the most loving Father of all—the very present help in trouble—carries us from despair to hope, from death to new life.

Other times, though, we experience a grief that doesn't correspond to anything we've done. It is simply a symptom or manifestation of a cursed world.

A mother who loses her child before its birth asks, "How long?" How long will her heart ache for her dear baby? A person who survives a car accident and is paralyzed for the rest of her life asks, "How long?" How long will she be devoid of physical feeling but filled with emotional pain?

It's not fair; it's not right. But it is life in this world, and this is how it's been since our father Adam and our mother Eve were driven out of Paradise. Utopia is an imaginary place. It is a land of make-believe. The real world does not work as it should. Every day that we rise from our beds is another day we will be tempted to despair of God's mercy.

This is why "How long?" has been a question on the lips of saints for thousands of years. "O Lord, how long shall I cry for help, and You will not hear?" asks Habakkuk, as he begins his book (1:2). "How long will the land mourn and the grass of every field wither?" asks Jeremiah as he watches Jerusalem, the chosen city of God, crumble around him (12:4). And "How long?" is the question the faithful martyrs of the Lord call out as they wait for

Rose

Him to exact justice and avenge their innocent blood (Revelation 6:9–10).

So what can I say? How can I respond to you and others in my life who ask, "How long?" What answer can I give myself when even my bones ache with the terrors of this painful world and my soul cries aloud to God? What answer comes to me at night when my whole being longs to escape this life of strife?

Well, maybe we should settle in and brace ourselves for a long ride. After all, Abraham waited a hundred years for his promised son. Israel sat in Egypt for four hundred years waiting for deliverance from bondage. It took thousands of years for the Savior to come after the promise was first made in Eden. And we've been waiting some two thousand years for the Messiah's second coming. How long? Sometimes *very* long.

In your despair, though, don't look down into the pit. If "very long" was the only answer I gave you, it would be incomplete. Peter has a different answer. He assures you that the Lord is not slow to fulfill His promise (2 Peter 3:9). Almost every preacher of significance throughout the years has thought the Lord's return is just around the corner. The people in Thessalonica quit their jobs, thinking Christ's return was imminent and it was no use to fill the last days by working! The Lord tells us we should be ever ready for His second coming. What could give us a greater cause for hope?

Whether you are suffering for a specific sin you've committed, then, or enduring the effects of a fallen world crashing down around you, look up—not down. Lift your eyes to the hills from which your help comes (Psalm 121). Look to the cross on the hill where Christ Himself suffered the wrath we deserved. His death and resurrection are the focal point of the best "never-ending story"—a true narrative of redemption and grace. It's not a fairy tale; it's quite real. And we are all a part of it through our Baptism into Christ.

But since the story is real, it is indeed filled with dark valleys of sorrow. Shelves topple over. People contract incurable diseases. Jets fly into skyscrapers, office buildings, and fields. The earth gives way and the mountains fall (Psalm 46:1–2). Life's a mess, but when we stand hopelessly and helplessly in the midst of tragedy, the most loving Father of all—the very present help in trouble—carries us from despair to hope, from death to new life. He even gives us a frequent foretaste of what is to come. Look to His perfect Son's body and blood in the Holy Supper and taste the forgiveness of sins and salvation that is yours now and for eternity. Carry your burdens to the altar. Gather with all His saints in heaven and here below and ask this: "How long, O Lord, will Your mercy endure?" He answers you in His Word and Sacraments: "Forever, My child. Forever."

Prayer: Heavenly Father, whose mercies are never ending, teach me through Your discipline that I might learn to love You more and so serve those around me. Help me during times of distress. Don't let me despair of Your grace. Preserve my body and soul and calm my languished heart with the faithfulness of Your promises. I pray in Christ's holy name. **Amen.**

Rose

monday

Personal Study Questions
Psalm 6:1–3

1. Psalm 6 is the first of several "Penitential Psalms" in the Psalter. (Scholars usually also include 32, 38, 51, 102, 130, and 143 in this category.) What phrases in the first three verses hint at the theme of repentance?

2. Think about a time when you, like the psalmist, feared God's discipline, His rebuke. What did you do? What helped you address your need?

3. How does Peter's answer in 2 Peter 3:9 help when you ask the psalmist's question "How long?" in response to the challenges you face today?

Rose

Psalm 6:4

Turn, O LORD, deliver my life;
save me for the sake of Your steadfast love.

Special Delivery

Americans have a strong sense of entitlement. Every day I find myself expecting a series of standard deliveries. I expect my alarm clock to deliver noise at the right time. I expect my breakfast to deliver energy until midday. I expect my car to deliver reliable transportation. I expect my diligence at work to deliver recognition. I expect my friends and family to deliver companionship. These expectations seem pretty normal to me. I don't ask for too much, do I? Since I tend to think these expectations are reasonable, you can imagine my level of discon-

Rose

tent when they're not fulfilled. A broken alarm clock leaves me late. A wimpy breakfast leaves me hungry. A car with a faulty transmission leaves me stranded. A lack of recognition at work leaves me bitter. A fair-weather friend leaves me lonely.

God has something to say about these delivery expectations:

> *And do not turn aside after empty things that cannot profit or deliver, for they are empty. For the* LORD *will not forsake His people, for His great name's sake, because it has pleased the* LORD *to make you a people for Himself. . . . Only fear the* LORD *and serve Him faithfully with all your heart. For consider what great things He has done for you.* 1 Samuel 12:21–22, 24

He calls these delivery systems in themselves empty and profitless. Ultimately, he calls us to recognize the presence of the *Deliverer* behind them all. We should see God at work, each and every time our clock wakes us, our breakfast fills us, our car moves us, our boss recognizes us, and our friends and family love us. He works through these to provide us with all our needs and many of our desires! Everything in this world is a gift. It is not, therefore, something we earn or deserve, but rather, something we receive from the good and gracious hand of our loving Creator who continues to sustain us in every need.

Ultimately, we should recognize that having things delivered to us is not what is most important in this life. Jesus tried to teach this to His followers, but it just didn't register with a lot of His hearers. Remember the young rich man who went away sad because he couldn't give up all his wealth? Think of the time when Christ spoke of freedom to Jewish believers in John 8. They laughed and said they were descendants of Abraham, never having been enslaved to anyone (v. 33). First of all, they really missed the boat if they honestly thought they'd never been slaves; didn't Egypt ring a bell? That aside, they failed to recognize the abstract variety of slavery Jesus was describing. Don't some of us lose

Rose

sight of that too? We live in a time and place where breakfast cereal is vitamin fortified and used cars come with hundred-thou-sand-mile warranties! We are free!

In truth, though, we are not. We are not truly free because our alarm clock wakes us in the morning or because our hard work earns us a promotion or a plaque on the wall. For what will it profit us if we gain the whole world and forfeit our souls? (Matthew 16:26). If we remain enslaved to our own sinful nature, we need a delivery not of goods but of our very person—of our very life.

The psalmist in verse 4 doesn't ask God to deliver him fame or wealth or personal happiness. Rather, the psalmist cries out that the Lord would deliver *him*. "Turn, O LORD, deliver my life." From whom or from what is he being delivered? He recognizes that because of his sin, he needs to be delivered from the damning consequences it brings—death itself. He needs to be delivered from the very depths of hell. He needs to be delivered from his own sinful flesh that still clings to his neck. He needs to be delivered from an eternal separation from his Creator.

The psalmist cries out for deliverance—a cry both of petition and of faith. He knows God will honor this request because it is in His very nature to do so.

What has the psalmist done, though, to be able to ask such a favor of the Lord? How can he be so bold? Has he not heard of reciprocity? Quid pro quo? We operate on an "I'll scratch your back if you scratch mine" basis. We help others either because they've helped us in the past or because we expect them to help us in the future. There is no such thing as a free lunch . . . right?

That may be how our society operates, but this would never stand up in God's court. John 3:16 is perhaps the clearest reminder of this. The world did not love God. The world had done nothing to earn His grace. Rather, God so loved the world that He gave His only Son.

The psalmist understood this. He didn't cry out for God to save him on account of anything he had done or anything he would do. Instead, he implored God's deliverance on the basis of

Rose

God's very being. "Save me for the sake of Your steadfast love" (Psalm 6:4). It's as though he is praying, "Save me, because this is what You do." More simply put: "Save me because You're You." The psalmist cries out for deliverance—a cry both of petition and of faith. He knows God will honor this request because it is in His very nature to do so. He doesn't ask that the Lord deliver earthly goods or worldly honor or physical release. Rather, he asks that the Lord deliver *him*. Period. And in so doing, he lets God be God.

Many times we are too preoccupied with what we want. Our prayers ask for all kinds of deliveries, omitting our own. This isn't all bad—because really, truly, we can ask anything of Him. As our Creator has promised, He gives us all we need and more in this life. But when, according to His gracious omniscience, He *doesn't* give us every single thing we ask for, let us never forget the fact that God delivered *us*. He delivered my life and yours.

Ironically, God's *own* delivery was a part of that pact. It wasn't quite as crass as mutual back scratching, but He did, in fact, make a deal. He sent an angel, Gabriel, to a young girl named Mary. He asked that virgin to be a part of His plan, and she accepted. She knew she wasn't worthy. Still, she understood that this was a part of God's sovereign preparation to save the world—not to reward humankind for anything they'd done, but rather to save them on account of His sheer unfailing, incomprehensible love. Although she didn't deserve it, and although we don't deserve it, Mary let God be God, and so must we. A sinner bore God so God could bear all of our sins. A human delivered Christ so Christ might deliver all of humanity.

And you—*you*, dear sister—are a part of that. Don't get so wrapped up in the standard deliveries of this world that you miss the best one of all: a humble virgin conceived and delivered Christ into a human life, and out of pure grace, He, God made man, delivered our lives eternally. This is how we are able and eager to deliver our love and service to those around us. We are merciful to others because our Father in heaven is merciful to us. He, in His infinite compassion, baptized us into His name. Rejoice in this, your most special delivery.

Rose

Prayer: Blessed Father in heaven, You who made the earth and sea and sky and all that is in them, You delivered me into this world through my physical birth, and You delivered me from this world through my spiritual rebirth in Baptism. You have promised always to tend to my needs. Keep filling my life with good things, Lord, and keep me free from the chains of sin and death so I might serve You with all love and gladness. Do this, as You've promised, on account of Your precious Son's perfect delivery, life, death, and resurrection. In His name and for His sake. *Amen.*

Rose

tuesday

Personal Study Questions
wPsalm 6:4

1. As you read verse 2 yesterday, you heard the psalmist plead for grace. He does not cite his past record of holiness or list the good things he has done for the Lord or His people. To what does he appeal instead?

2. Now, in verse 4, he adds a second reason for which he turns to the Lord for deliverance. What is it?

3. In addition to delivering you from sin, fear, and death, what other blessings has your Lord delivered already today? How will you thank Him for them and use them to honor Him?

Rose

Psalm 6:5

*For in death there
is no remembrance of You;
in Sheol who will give You praise?*

Down with Death

Death is one of those things I'd rather not think about, and I would *certainly* rather not write about. Unfortunately, though, there are frequent reminders that death, like taxes, cannot be avoided. These reminders come in various forms. My introduction to this concept was the flushing of a deceased goldfish, whose name now escapes me. Things went downhill from there. Next, a frog named Jim, then a bird named Sydney, and eventually, the compounding of loss climaxed in the death of human beings I loved and still miss—a dear childhood friend, a great-aunt, a godmother. I'd like to forget the pain of these deaths, but that's impossible.

Rose

There are more subtle reminders, too, of death and its crouched position not so very far from my own beating heart. Runner's knee alone is enough to remind me of my mortality. Wrinkles are starting to gather around the corners of my eyes. A few stray grays look distinguished on my husband but do not hold the same appeal when I sport them myself.

In confirmation class, our pastor taught us Newton's second law of thermodynamics: all processes go in one direction, and that direction is down. In other words, everything is in a constant state of decay. Even as I type this, I might as well acknowledge that from this very moment until the day I die, I will never be as young as I am right now. By the time you read these words, my joint pain and crow's-feet and gray hair will undoubtedly have increased. If that doesn't hit home, consider this: as you read these words, you are living the youngest moment of your remaining life. Modern scientists try to develop remedies for all of these issues. Skin-firming lotions, core-strengthening exercises, and energy-building vitamins will put you back on the track to youthfulness. Or will they? It seems a little silly if you consider that we are engaged in combat against the laws of physics. We are denying the inevitable.

The psalmist certainly senses death's closeness as he laments his own sinful plight and cries out to the Lord. In the previous verse, he asked God to deliver his life. Here in verse 5 he demonstrates that he knows what the alternative is. He concedes in plain language that he, like all creatures and processes, is on the path to decay. He doesn't candy-coat it or make it sound pleasant because he knows it is not. This is why he writes, "For in death there is no remembrance of You; in Sheol who will give You praise?" You're probably wondering where the silver lining is. Look all you like, but if you take this verse as it stands, isolated as it is, you will find none.

It is easy and tempting to take a psalm like this one, a psalm of lamentation and contrition, and spiritualize it into something it is not. We are tempted to read a verse like this and say, "Oh, the psalmist didn't *actually* mean that. . . . " We would like to

Rose

sweeten it a bit so it doesn't sound as disturbing or as morbid or as fatalistic. Really, this is no different from what we do with our anti-aging treatments. If we can ward off wrinkled skin, we feel as though we are warding off death itself. We're fooling ourselves.

What I admire about David's discussion of death is that he calls it what it is. He asks, "who in Sheol will give you praise?" During the time of the Old Testament, Sheol was understood as a sort of underworld inhabited by the deceased. Other patriarchs (such as Joseph's father, Jacob) spoke of going there. In those days, believers understood that when they died they would descend into the depths.

In Psalm 6:5, David makes it quite clear that a decomposing body simply does not have the physical capacity to give praise to the Lord. Lungs emptied of oxygen and vocal chords muted by death cannot magnify God's holy name. He knew he was destined for the grave, just as all of us know in our hearts. David did not try to over-spiritualize the reality of death. He didn't pretend it was all fine and dandy.

Interestingly, Peter's sermon at Pentecost (recorded in Acts 2) confirmed everything the psalmist had foreseen thousands of years earlier. Addressing the crowd before him, Peter said, "Brothers, I may say to you with confidence about the patriarch David that he both died and was buried, and his tomb is with us to this day" (v. 29). In speaking this way, Peter plainly acknowledged the reality of death. A tomb—a physical place—contained the dusty remains of the once-living, breathing writer of Psalm 6. And did those dusty remains give praise? No. There was no breath in those lifeless particles.

However, this is not the end of the story. Peter goes on to remind his hearers that David did not die without hope. His soul rests in Abraham's bosom, along with all the other sleeping saints, clinging to the hope of the resurrection of the dead. While his soul praised God in heaven, he awaited the Last Day when he would praise God again with his own lips, tongue, and lungs. He knew the reality of death, yet he did not despair in the face of it. Rather, David trusted God's oath to him and believed that one of his de-

Rose

scendants, the promised Messiah, would conquer hades itself and would claim for His kingdom all those belonging to the covenant. David's Offspring, the tender shoot promised by the Lord, would not decay in a tomb as David would. This Messiah, who we now know is Jesus Christ, did not remain in His tomb forever. Having suffered for our sins on the cross, He rose again on the third day. Jesus did not remain in His tomb, and neither will David, and neither will you.

That death still grieves us is a simple testament to the fact that it was not a part of the Creator's original plan. God did not design a world in a state of decay. This current condition was brought on by sin—Adam and Eve's sin, and, ultimately, your sin and mine. We inherited the blame for the fallen reality in which we live. Death is the culmination of this fall. Apart from Christ, there is no remembrance of God in death, and there is no praise for Him wafting up from our shadowy tombs. While David trusted the promise, it had not yet been fulfilled. Christ had not yet been born of a virgin, suffered under Pontius Pilate, crucified, buried, and raised.

Unlike David, we live on the other side of Christ's first coming. Christ's resurrection from the dead and His glorious return for us on the Last Day give us hope. His resurrection means also the resurrection in perfection of the great saints before Him who died in faith. And it means for us that the grave will not mute our voices forever.

Anti-aging products will not stop death. They cannot. And although your skin will wrinkle and your voice will become raspy, remember this: Christ's victory will be yours. On the final day, we will be raised from the dusty tombs. Our skin will be resplendent and new, and we will be given a renovated set of vocal chords, which will indeed praise the Lord for all eternity. When Christ descended into the depths of hell, He could have waved a banner that read, "Down with Death," for this is precisely what He accomplished through His resurrection victory. He accomplished for you what no scientist could. He reversed your constant state of decay. Let all that has breath praise the Lord!

Rose

Prayer: Holy God, who made a perfect world, forgive me for falling away from Your grace. The wages of my sin is death, and this cannot be avoided, but You, through Your Son, conquered the grave. By Your Holy Spirit, I have faith and hope in Your promise that death will not hold me. Comfort me daily with this truth so I might cling to You and give praise to You in all I say and do. In the name of Jesus Christ, our Lord, **Amen.**

Rose

wednesday

Personal Study Questions
Psalm 6:5

1. The psalmist, David, senses his guilt so deeply that he fears it may kill him! How does verse 5 indicate this?

2. "Few people today take their sin this seriously." Would you agree with that statement? Tell why you think so.

3. Has your own guilt ever troubled you this deeply? Why or why not?

4. How does today's faith narrative connect Acts 2 to today's psalm verse to form a Good News response to the bad news sin and death bring into our lives?

Rose

Psalm 6:6–7

I am weary with my moaning;
every night I flood my bed with tears;
I drench my couch with my weeping.
My eye wastes away because of grief; it
grows weak because of all my foes.

Good Grief

I was a pretty bad kid when it came to cleaning my room. I remember one time I had to get it all picked up so I could go to a friend's house. Naturally I tried every child's time-tested, foolproof plan—shove everything under the bed. Sadly for me, my parents were too well versed in childish ploys to leave this convenient space unchecked. "Good grief, Rosie," they sighed, "do you think that's any way to deal with the problem?" Grounding me was their sentence; loud lamentations and abundant tears, my response.

I didn't like cleaning my room then and I don't like it now. I'm twenty-six years old, and to this day, I'd rather

Rose

shove everything under my bed than sort it, organize it, and stow it properly. It's just a lot easier to put it out of sight and worry about it some other time. Out of sight, out of mind.

Sin is one of those things that many of us brush off and shove aside. Sure, we pay lip service to being sinners. After all, we've been raised on a steady diet of shoulds, musts, and don'ts. We know what sin is and what it does. We get it. Yet we merely nod our heads with artificial piety when the preacher bellows the full severity of the Law in our direction on Sunday morning. We speak the words of corporate confession and state that we have been sinful in our thoughts, words, and deeds, but we figure the person in the pew next to us has done a lot worse. Overall, when I reflect on my sins of the day, my list comes up pretty short.

I lost my patience a time or two . . . but who hasn't? I showed up for work late and left early . . . but I do more than anyone else there anyway. I failed to call my friend in need . . . but I have my own problems to deal with. I didn't read anything from Scripture . . . but who has time? I used the Lord's name in vain . . . but He knows I didn't mean it. I bad-mouthed my neighbors . . . but did you hear how loud their music was last night?

With every *but* I take my sin and put it under the bed. And if you're anything like me, you've done the same a time or two. Along with the Pharisee of Luke 18, we are confident of our own righteousness. We thank God that we're not like those really bad sinners we see on the news or in the tabloids. Instead, beating our chest and begging for mercy like the penitent tax collector, we pat ourselves on the back and beg for recognition.

The psalmist, however, did no such thing. He wrote in Psalm 6:6–7: "I am weary with my moaning; every night I flood my bed with tears; I drench my couch with my weeping. My eye wastes away because of grief; it grows weak because of all my foes." He felt the full, overwhelming weight of his sins. He knew that in addition to his very real enemies pressing in on every side, he himself—his own sinful nature—was perhaps the strongest of them all! Instead of shoving his sins under the bed, he poured them out before the Lord. And as he did, his bed was transformed. No lon-

Rose

135

ger was it a fort under which to hide secret sins. Rather, it was a sponge saturated with tears, drenched through and through.

Children are better at understanding this kind of grief. When they do something wrong, they realize the heaviness of their sin. They understand what it means to grow weary with moaning. I remember working at a day-care facility and observing how a child who was being disciplined would eventually tire from the effort required of tears. Finally the little one would gasp, too worn out to squeeze out one more tear.

When the terror of our sin finally catches up with us, Jesus is there alongside us, bearing the pain. He was without any sin of His own, but He willingly took upon Himself the sin of the entire world. All that was hidden under beds and in closets and behind closed doors was felt in His broken body nailed to the cross.

As adults, though, it is rare for us to reach this point. We are either clever enough to avoid the consequences of our sins or jaded enough not to be bothered by them. We downplay our faults and call attention to our strengths. When we cry, we do so because of some unmet want or need, not because we are heartily sorry for our sins.

Our Father in heaven sees our stubborn pride. He knows all of the childish tactics we employ to look good in our own eyes and the eyes of our neighbors. He sees right through the façade. Every time we take a posture of might rather than meekness, we attempt to justify our sinful ways and stow them away, under our beds and out of our heads. Eventually, though, it gets pretty crowded under there. Finally our eyes grow weak—not necessarily because of grief, but on account of denial. We tire of turning the blind eye to all the rotten stuff shoved out of sight. There's not enough room to hold all of our shames and guilt and offenses. Sooner or later, the haunting collection keeps us up at night with the hideous beating of our own telltale heart. We lie awake with the paralyzing terror that true knowledge of sin incites and real contrition rouses.

Only when our sin drives us to misery do we finally cry out. Only then do we realize the fullness of our depravity. Only then do we kneel with our head cradled in our hands and our sins heavy in our heart. And to be frank, it is something to cry about, precise-

Rose

ly because we can't deal with the problem of sin. Not on our own. We finally feel the deep woe of the psalmist.

Christ Himself understands our suffering. When the terror of our sin finally catches up with us, Jesus is beside us, bearing the pain. He didn't have a soft bed to cry into on the night when He was betrayed. He cried into the soil of the Garden of Gethsemane. He knelt on the hard ground and sweated blood contemplating the bitter cup before Him. He was without any sin of His own, but He willingly took upon Himself the sin of the entire world. All that was hidden under beds and in closets and behind closed doors was felt in His broken body nailed to the cross—on display for all the world to see.

This was good grief; this was perfect grief. He went to such great lengths to restore, heal, and pardon us. When we kneel with the psalmist and confess our sins with heartfelt repentance, and when our eyes grow weak with pain and suffering, our Lord promises that the sorrow will last only the night. Hope and joy come with the morning. Maybe not tomorrow morning, or the next, but when the dawn of His second coming is upon us, we will surely rejoice in the rays of His victory and the coming of His heavenly kingdom where our tears will be wiped away forever.

Prayer: Dear Lord, whose Son suffered beyond compare, forgive me for acting as though my sins do not matter. Forgive me for despising You and disregarding the needs of those around me. Do not forsake me for my pharisaical attitudes, but look on me with grace. See me through the light of Christ's resurrection so my own dark and weary eyes might see You in my neighbor and serve You in them. Thank You for Your unfailing forgiveness and the sure promise that my sorrow and sighing will cease. In Jesus' name I pray. **Amen.**

Rose

Personal Study Questions
Psalm 6:6–7

1. Today's faith narrative notes, "Every time we take a posture of might rather than meekness, we attempt to justify our sinful ways and stow them away, under our beds and out of our heads. Eventually, though, it gets pretty crowded under there." When have you experienced this in your own life?

2. In verses 6–7, David expresses the depth of his anguish in a way different from his earlier words. How so?

3. To what do you attribute the deep anguish the psalmist is experiencing?

4. Which words from today's faith narrative bring the comfort of the Gospel to your heart? What will you say to your Savior in light of His forgiveness and steadfast love?

Psalm 6:8–10

Depart from me, all you workers of evil, for the LORD has heard the sound of my weeping. The LORD has heard my plea; the LORD accepts my prayer. All my enemies shall be ashamed and greatly troubled; they shall turn back and be put to shame in a moment.

You Have My Word

One of my students approached me quite some time ago with a request to do something on her behalf. "Of course," I replied, "I'll get right on that. You have my word." I had every good intention of doing what I'd promised. Weeks turned into months, and her petition got lost in the shuffle of day-to-day life. I was so busy; there were phone calls, e-mails, and stacks of papers. I didn't mean to be negligent or uncaring; I simply forgot to act on my word. One night, I realized I hadn't taken care of it. The next day I apologized. I told her my promise to help had slipped my mind and assured her I would follow through. "That's

Rose

139

all right," she said. "Someone else took care of it." I felt terrible. I let her down. She had to seek help elsewhere because I failed her.

Many times we are disappointed by those around us who fall short of our expectations. We feel betrayed when those we love don't keep a promise. I have been on both sides. I'm not the only one who has felt the sting of abandonment by a boyfriend who promised his love and affection. I would ask, "Do you love me?" and his answer was always a convincing yes. He gave me his word. But young love is a fanciful thing. And in time, it became apparent that his resolve didn't equal his sentiment.

When we're disappointed and hurt by others, we look for another source of comfort. We want to feel better or we want to feel numb—what we *don't* want to feel is bad. There are all kinds of remedies for the woman scorned. Retail therapy is one of my vices of choice. But if extravagant spending isn't your preferred method of self-consolation, there are other options. Sexual impropriety might be your poison. Perhaps excessive drinking or the misuse of legal drugs. Or maybe you try to regain a sense of control by inflicting some form of bodily harm on yourself, like under- or overeating. Maybe you lash out at others to soothe your own hurting heart. Whatever the balm, you have probably realized that it comes up short every single time. When others let us down, no matter what we do to pick ourselves back up, we still feel low. And eventually, we can become so calloused and bruised that we stop asking others for help and rely wholly upon ourselves.

Self-sufficient women can have four pots on the stove at one time without one burnt bottom. They can manage the tenuous balance of children and a career. They can carry five bags of groceries in one hand and still unlock the door. They can do it all without help, thank you very much! Or can I? Or can you?

In truth, we are incapable of self-sufficiency. We need others. Yet we resist them because coupled with their love is the constant threat of disappointment. And at times, we even reject God because if everyone else has let us down, who's to say He won't?

Of all the people in Scripture, perhaps Job felt this ache more than any other. You've probably heard the story. The head-

Rose

line could go something like "The man who had it all lost it all—
left with nothing." Pictured would be a shot of the once-great,
now-pathetic man without property, children, or health. Even his
friends turned against him. And oh, how he cried! He sat with
boils on his skin and ash on his face. He wallowed in the despair
of true grief. He lamented his own birth. Yet he did not curse God.

How did he not? Why did he not? Job clung to a confidence
outside of human capability and beyond human reason. In the
face of adversaries beyond imagination, he replied, "I know that
my Redeemer lives." That Redeemer hadn't yet been born, but He
was promised. He was to save us all—from others who fail us and
from our own selves that disappoint us just as much if not more.
The Redeemer in whom Job placed his trust was Jesus Christ.

And in fact, Christ in the flesh knew rejection and despair
even more than Job did. He was mocked and disrespected in His
own town. His followers left Him when He was taken to trial.
Even His friend Peter pretended to not know Him. As Isaiah puts
it, "He was despised and rejected by men; a man of sorrows, and
acquainted with grief" (53:3a). At His darkest moment, His own
Father forsook Him. He cried from the cross, "My God, My God,
why have You forsaken Me?" This was not a metaphor. This was
not a poetic interpretation of what was going on. This was real.

Sure—Jesus' hometown and His followers and His friends
and even His own Father abandoned Him. But we let ourselves off
the hook. *We* would never let Him down. Ah, how foolish we are to
think that our good intentions are enough. Isaiah continues, "and
as one from whom men hide their faces He was despised, and we
esteemed Him not" (53:3). That's right—*we* esteemed him not. I
esteemed Him not; you esteemed Him not.

As much as I regretted having let down my student, how
much graver is it to fail to esteem Christ? How can I possibly cry
out to Him when I have grieved Him so deeply by my offenses
and transgressions? The answer is found in Psalm 6. David spent
the entire psalm lamenting his sinful flesh. He pleaded that God
not rebuke him in His anger. He asked God how long he would
have to endure the pain of his sin. He begged to be delivered. He

Rose

soaked his bed with tears that sprung from the knowledge of his own corrupted body and soul that failed to fear, love, and trust in God. And in the end, he, like Job, placed his trust in the Lord.

Before the prayer is even on his lips, he is confident that it is heard and answered. Thus he writes, "Depart from me, all you workers of evil, for the LORD has heard the sound of my weeping. The LORD has heard my plea; the LORD accepts my prayer. All my enemies shall be ashamed and greatly troubled; they shall turn back and be put to shame in a moment." What confidence he has, to trust so fully in the faithfulness of God.

My student put her confidence in me, and I disappointed her. I put my confidence in a relationship, and it disappointed me. We are all let down by others. And we are all guilty of doing the same. But thanks be to God, we are not without an Arbiter. And He will come again to judge both the living and the dead. He will look upon us and not see our failures. He won't point an accusing finger for having abandoned Him time after time while chasing after our own sinful desires. Instead, He will rule in our favor. We have God's Word, lasting and true. And by that Word, the Word made flesh, Christ Himself, we will have eternal victory over our fiercest foes and greatest enemies: sin, death, and the power of the devil.

Prayer: Father in heaven, whose love never fails, hear my plea and accept my prayer as You accepted David's. Forgive me, Lord, for failing others. Forgive me, Lord, for failing You. Give me a new dose of my baptismal grace every morning. Cover me again in the faithful promise of Your water joined with the Word so I might live as Your child in all I say and do. In the holy name of Jesus, who declares me righteous for His sake. *Amen.*

Rose

Friday

Personal Study Questions
Psalm 6:8–10

1. Today's faith narrative begins by focusing on disappointment, on how easily we let others down, even when we don't intend to, and on the temptation to believe that our Lord might similarly disappoint us. When have you found yourself falling for that temptation?

2. Verses 8–10 express the psalmist's relief as he relies on the Lord's faithfulness. What phrases from these verses seem especially powerful to you in this regard?

3. How do the phrases you mentioned also describe your relief in Jesus' forgiveness?

Rose

Group Bible Study for Week 4
Psalm 6

1. Psalm 6 is often included in the category of "Penitential Psalms." Others that are often included in this category are Psalms 32, 38, 51, 102, 130, and 143. If your group is large enough, divide into six groups and assign a different psalm from this list to each group. If not, choose one of the psalms from this list for the whole group to examine in more depth, using these questions:

   a. In what ways is the psalm you chose similar to Psalm 6?
   (List all the similarities you can.)

   b. In what ways does the psalm you chose differ from Psalm 6? (List all the differences you can.)

   c. When might you pray either Psalm 6 or the second penitential psalm you have considered?

   d. What words from either psalm do you find especially comforting? Share your answer with a partner and explain why you chose the words you did.

2. When we pray for mercy, we ask that God will not inflict the penalty we deserve. When we pray for grace, we ask that God will give us the blessings we do not deserve, including the blessing of forgiveness. Which verses in Psalm 6 plead for mercy? Which ask for grace?

3. In some senses, the distinction between mercy and grace doesn't really matter that much. However, remembering it may deepen our prayer lives. How might that happen?

4. As David grieves over his sins in verses 6–7, his grief deepens as he considers "all [his] foes." Who would these be? Why would remembering them grieve him even more?

5. Look through your hymnal to find the section that includes hymns of confession. In what ways are the thoughts expressed in those hymns similar to David's thoughts in Psalm 6?

6. Sometimes God's people have trouble "feeling" forgiven even after they have confessed their sins. They may believe their sin is too big. They may anguish over the many times they have repeated a particular vice (habit sin). They may remember "knowing better" and going ahead anyway, despite the warnings God gave them by means of their conscience. What would you tell a friend who shared feelings of guilt and its anguish with you?

7. In light of the truths of this psalm, how would you like your life from now on to be different? What will you ask the Holy Spirit to do *for* you and *in* you so those changes come about?

8. The prayers from this week's faith narratives spoke with special eloquence. Which did you find especially meaningful or instructive? Explain.

Psalm 7

For those who are falsely accused

¹ O Lᴏʀᴅ my God, in You do I take refuge;
save me from all my pursuers and deliver me,

² lest like a lion they tear my soul apart,
rending it in pieces, with none to deliver.

³ O Lᴏʀᴅ my God, if I have done this,
if there is wrong in my hands,

⁴ if I have repaid my friend with evil
or plundered my enemy without cause,

⁵ let the enemy pursue my soul and overtake it,
and let him trample my life to the ground
and lay my glory in the dust. *Selah*

⁶ Arise, O Lᴏʀᴅ, in Your anger;
lift Yourself up against the fury of my enemies;
awake for me; You have appointed a judgment.

⁷ Let the assembly of the peoples be gathered about You;
over it return on high.

⁸ The Lᴏʀᴅ judges the peoples;
judge me, O Lᴏʀᴅ, according to my righteousness
and according to the integrity that is in me.

⁹ Oh, let the evil of the wicked come to an end,
and may You establish the righteous—
You who test the minds and hearts,

O righteous God!

¹⁰ My shield is with God,
who saves the upright in heart.

¹¹ God is a righteous judge,
and a God who feels indignation every day.

¹² If a man does not repent, God will whet His sword;
He has bent and readied His bow;

¹³ He has prepared for him His deadly weapons,
making His arrows fiery shafts.

¹⁴ Behold, the wicked man conceives evil
and is pregnant with mischief
and gives birth to lies.

¹⁵ He makes a pit, digging it out,
and falls into the hole that he has made.

¹⁶ His mischief returns upon his own head,
and on his own skull his violence descends.

¹⁷ I will give to the LORD the thanks due to His righteousness,
and I will sing praise to the name of the LORD, the Most High.

Terry Lee Kieschnick

Psalm 7:1–5

O LORD my God, in You do I take refuge; save me from all my pursuers and deliver me, lest like a lion they tear my soul apart, rending it in pieces, with none to deliver. O LORD my God, if I have done this, if there is wrong in my hands, if I have repaid my friend with evil or plundered my enemy without cause, let the enemy pursue my soul and overtake it, and let him trample my life to the ground and lay my glory in the dust. Selah

A Secret Place

Help! Help! Calgon, take me away! Ever had that feeling? Are there days when you wish someone or something could take you away to a secret place for just a few hours? Maybe you feel like you are drowning in the sea of life. Your life swirls out of control and every-

where you turn, someone wants something from you.

I know that feeling.

I was not aware that my life was about to undergo rapid, dramatic change. My life thus far had consisted in raising our children, managing a wholesale fine-jewelry store, and being the wife of a pastor who later was a district president. Our lives changed in eight seconds flat when he was elected president of The Lutheran Church—Missouri Synod. My heart was filled with monumental joy that Jerry had been elected. Yet I also felt fear at the thought of moving to St. Louis, leaving family behind in Texas, finding a new home, meeting new friends, and sharing a new calling. I wasn't sure I could live up to the expectations the people of our church body might have of me. I feared that I wouldn't have the right answers, that I didn't know Scripture well enough, and, heaven forbid, that I would have to speak in front of groups that were much different from my previous audiences. As tears fell down my cheeks, I remembered God's promise that He would never leave me or forsake me in this new chapter of my life. He was and is truly my refuge and strength.

The summer after I was in the seventh grade, my friend Lynn and I were invited to go swimming in Lake Austin. Texas is very hot that time of year, so when we went in the lake to splash and play, the water felt cool and refreshing. After a while, we swam out a little farther from shore. We were enjoying the sun on our faces and backs when, suddenly, Lynn grabbed the hair on the back of my head and began to pull me under. I hadn't known that my friend was not a good swimmer. She was trying to climb on top of me to get air, and she panicked as she feared she would drown. She was not a lion as described in our psalm (v. 2), yet her arms felt like strong paws around me. I feared I would be ripped to pieces and we would both drown. No one would rescue us; anyone watching undoubtedly would think we were having a grand time playing. I prayed, "Please, God, help me keep my cool and get us to shore safely."

Somehow, God gave me the strength and the will to break free of Lynn's hold and come up for air. The first breath to fill my throbbing lungs was unforgettable and glorious! Between gasps of air, I told Lynn I would help her, but I also pleaded with her to calm down, which was critical if we were going to survive. We swam closer to shore, and when our feet finally felt the lake bed, Lynn began to cry. She tearfully expressed how sorry she was that she had panicked; she really was afraid of deep water, and she had been petrified when she was unable to touch the bottom. I cried tears of joy because we were safe. God had rescued us. That day, I became aware of how precious life and breath are. I was so thankful that God had graciously spared our lives.

No matter what evil, wicked, or perverted plans the devil has in mind for us, our refuge is in God, who assures us that He is always with us to take care of the problem.

Why is it that we wait until we feel threatened or frightened to call upon God to rescue us from the evils of this world? We plead for Him to help us through all the little pestering fears that come our way day and night, fears that seem to drain the life out of us and steal our joy. We believe that if God will just rescue us "this time," we will be happy, joyful, and relieved. But it seems that as soon as God saves us, something else comes along from which we need to be rescued. Somehow it is hard to let go of our self-reliance and let God help us each and every day. We are a "do it ourselves" people. It is so difficult sometimes to commit our lives to our heavenly Father and to cast our burdens upon Him.

When we are faced with foes, fears, and problems that threaten to take hold and destroy us, our only remedy is to seek God and to find our refuge in Him. We rightly pray, "Lord, rescue me from whatever is pursuing me." The devil walks about like a roaring lion, seeking to devour us at each moment of our lives; he wants nothing more than to drag us off to eternal damnation. No matter what evil, wicked, or perverted plans the devil has in mind for us, God is our refuge, who assures us that He is always with us to take care of our problems. He is there for us 24/7—no need to make an appointment, stand in line, or take a number!

This refuge is where we can hide and where the devil cannot touch us. It is a special place where we can go when we are hurting, overwhelmed, or fearful. There are times when we are mistreated, persecuted, and overburdened, even to the point that we think we can't take it anymore. When we feel this way, our dear, heavenly Father wants us to come to Him. We can be certain that He is there with open and outstretched arms, assuring us of His stable, special, and soothing protection.

God has been my refuge and strength throughout all of my life, especially in recent years. When asked to represent our church body in various settings, many of which were outside my comfort zone, I feared that each time I spoke, some things might be misunderstood or taken out of context. That might not have been as serious or life threatening as a lion ripping me to pieces as the psalmist describes in verse 2, but I needed my "safe place" when I was feeling anxious and afraid. As long as God helped me to seek His will and guidance and not to try to do everything myself, things would work out to His glory.

I am very passionate and care deeply for others. I have great concern for the welfare of people, especially the other women of our church body. I still struggle with how best to encourage, love, share with, and care for them, and I wrestle with the challenge of leading more people to Jesus and His phenomenal love. Yet, each day, as I place my trust in God and ask Him to give me the courage to witness honestly and openly, He continues to open doors for me to do so in the light of His eternal love. Strengthened through God's Word and Sacraments, I am free, and so are you, to share with others the light of Christ's love.

A Scripture passage that keeps me from being discouraged is Joshua 1:9: "'Have I not commanded you? Be strong and courageous. Do not be frightened, and do not be dismayed, for the LORD your God is with you wherever you go.'" By God's grace and with an understanding husband, I am no longer fearful of my role in representing our church body. I feel blessed and honored at each opportunity. Although my knees still knock, I am deeply humbled to be asked to speak in public. I do so, praying for God's guidance.

As we live our lives, we pray that our thoughts, words, and deeds will be to His glory. We are reminded in Colossians 3:23, "Whatever you do, work heartily, as for the Lord and not for men."

Do things that are uncomfortable if God leads you there.

Terry

We serve the Lord. We don't need to look only for earthly places of refuge but also for a heavenly one. Through Jesus' saving death on the cross for our sin-stained souls, He provides a safe place not only in this life, but also in the life to come—heaven, where we will be forever with Him. To God be the glory!

Prayer: Dearest Father, thank You for caring for us each and every hour of the day and for assuring us beyond all doubt that we can go to You whenever we fear we are being pursued by the "lions" of this world. Whatever the perils, the pitfalls, and the pains that come into our lives, You are our constant Companion, Protector, and Savior. We are grateful that in Your mercy, You provide a refuge. Help us to look for and be aware of those who are drowning in this world and in need of Your comforting words and saving grace. This we pray in the precious name of Jesus Christ, Your Son, our Lord and Savior. **Amen.**

Terry

monday

Personal Study Questions
Psalm 7:1–5

1. Today's faith narrative describes a time in which the author nearly drowned. What clues in the first verses of Psalm 7 lead you to believe that the psalm's author, David, experienced similar panic? *V2, V5*

2. Scholars believe that David wrote this psalm as he escaped the murderous, treasonous plot of his own son Absalom. In addition to the fear, disbelief, and uncertainty that arose in his heart, David also faced—perhaps for the first time—the fact that others besides Absalom opposed his rule. Shimei, for example, used this opportunity to make public his true feelings. (See 2 Samuel 16:5–8.) Bible scholars, including the reformer Martin Luther, have connected Psalm 7 with this incident in David's life. Why do you think they may have done so?

3. When have you "fought lions," experiencing the kind of unfounded accusations that threatened to shred your heart? How do David's words mirror your feelings? *Sounds like he's been king for awhile; He sounds desperate; talks about friends and enemies*

4. As 2 Samuel 16:9–14 makes clear, David did not take revenge, although he could easily have ordered Shimei's execution. Instead, verse 14 tells us that at the Jordan River, David "refreshed himself." (See also 2 Samuel 19:16–21 and 1 Kings 2:8–9.)

   a. How might praying the prayer that became Psalm 7 have refreshed David? *He reminds himself who's in control of the end results, and the destiny of evil*

   b. How might praying this prayer during times of false accusation and gossip refresh you? *Same! Puts focus back on God, His wisdom, mercy, omniscience, justice*

Terry

Psalm 7:6–7

*Arise, O LORD, in Your anger; lift Yourself up against
the fury of my enemies; awake for me; You have
appointed a judgment. Let the assembly of the peoples
be gathered about You; over it return on high.*

Deliver Us
from Evil

Reading Psalm 7:6 is difficult for me
as a Christian woman. It's hard to
imagine actually asking God to rise
up against the rage of our enemies.
Yet, in a very real way, that is truly
powerful and very comforting to
know!

We don't want to admit that
we have enemies. Doesn't everyone want to be loved
and cherished? But, because of sin, we do have enemies
and oppressors in all shapes and forms—not only living,
breathing persons, but also unhealthy habits, addictions,

Terry

154

abuses, hurts, fears, and temptations. We become very good at repressing and denying to the world (and to ourselves) how we feel about these enemies—until one day, something or someone triggers those deep, dark feelings and they take hold of us. That's when we begin to live in the darkness of denial and despair, thinking we are getting away with our "li'l secrets" and that no one will be the wiser. Yet, we cannot go forward into God's light until we accept our faults and failures and ask for His help to turn away from them.

Does the saying "time heals all wounds" sound familiar? Maybe it is true for some, but many of us are unable to allow healing to take place. The wound festers and spreads and, if left unattended, consumes our thoughts and actions.

Our vicarage year in Charlotte, North Carolina, proved to be a memorable and monumental time for Jerry and for me. I worked in the church office and also at a women's boutique. The Tweed Shop had a lovely atmosphere of antiques and nooks that provided places to display beautiful clothing, shoes, and accessories. The store was an upscale haven to business women and ladies who had the means to purchase all the fashion firsts displayed there.

Mr. Ashcraft and his wife, Laura, had established the business—a dream come true for them. Tragically, she was killed in a car accident only two years after the store opened. A beautiful portrait of her, complete with a bronze plaque professing her love for her faith, family, and fashion, hung on one of the walls in the shop. Working there was a wonderful experience for me. I enjoyed designing and decorating the store's front windows and helping customers make just the right selections. During that year, I learned much about life, myself, and the retail world.

One of the ladies who came in with great regularity was Kit. She had an arresting sense of style and charm and had been a dear friend of the Ashcrafts for many years. Kit was a very successful realtor. Always in a hurry and moving at a hectic pace, Kit would come into the Tweed Shop like a tornado, picking up loads of clothes and accessories in her path. Deciding on outfits to take with her didn't take her long. However, she would leave mounds of

Terry

clothing in the dressing room after her departure.

One day, Kit breezed in "needing" a new outfit for a gala she was attending that evening. Dresses and shoes were pulled from racks and stacked in the dressing room. As she perused the accessories, she asked me to show her a pair of expensive earrings sitting on a shelf in a display case. I pulled out the earrings and excused myself to ring up a purchase for another customer. Kit continued trying on many outfits and shoes, finally deciding on what would work for this particular evening's event. As usual, we hurriedly rang up her sales, and she dashed out the door at full speed. After picking up all the discarded dresses and shoes and returning them to their proper places, I remembered the earrings. I rushed to the display case—maybe Kit had returned them to the proper shelf. She hadn't. I searched the dressing room frantically—no earrings! Maybe they were at the checkout counter if she had decided she didn't need them. Not! Surely there was an explanation for this dilemma. My heart sank. I didn't want to believe that someone like Kit was capable of taking these very valuable jewels.

Each day we start fresh by asking our dear heavenly Father to lead us not into temptation but to deliver us from evil. It is only by God's grace that we can ask Him to wage war against our enemies— Satan, the world, and our own sinful flesh.

Friday was my day to help Mr. Ashcraft count the money, clean up, and close the store. At first, I was tempted to say nothing about the expensive earrings. I hoped that they would turn up or that Kit would return them after finding them mixed in with the clothing she had purchased. However, I just couldn't let go of the uneasy feeling in my heart. With much fear and trepidation, I asked Mr. Ashcraft if he had just a few minutes, as I needed to discuss something with him. I proceeded to tell him how Kit had rushed in to buy something for the gala.

He smiled, chuckled, and said, "Yes, that's Kit!" Knowing that they were very good friends, it was hard for me to speak up about the earrings. My heart was heavy and beating fast as the words tumbled out of my mouth: "I am so sorry that I can't find them anywhere. I have checked with all the other sales associates to see if by chance they have seen the earrings, or if perhaps Kit

Terry

has called or had come back to purchase them while I was away from the store for dinner. I felt it was my duty to tell you since I was the one who took them from the case and showed them to her. I take full responsibility for this loss and will pay for them, but it will take a long time to do so."

Mr. Ashcraft was very understanding. "Thank you for coming forward and telling me," he said. "I appreciate your concern about the expensive earrings and wanting to pay for them, but I don't hold you responsible for what happened today. People aren't always what they seem, and sometimes they can fool you." At that moment, I felt relief for telling him, but concern for the years Kit and the Ashcrafts had been friends. I hoped it was all a misunderstanding. As I was leaving the Tweed Shop to go home that evening, Mr. Ashcraft stopped and said to me, "Terry, don't ever apologize for being honest, caring, and a good steward of my shop. I knew she took the earrings, as I was coming out of my office and saw her put them in her bag. This wasn't the first time. But she will no longer have the privilege of shopping here."

I was flabbergasted and speechless! All I could think of was that Kit had it all; why would she risk ruining a friendship—and facing prosecution—by taking a pair of earrings she could well afford to buy? As I left the shop that evening, I wondered why God had chosen to put me in this position, to have me meet Kit, and to tell Mr. Ashcraft what I had seen. Yet I was grateful that He had touched my heart to speak up. And I prayed that God would help Kit "rise up against the rage" of whatever "enemies" possessed her to shoplift.

We are often powerless against the enemies that cause us to fall into many kinds of sin, at times causing our lives to unravel. Psalm 38:4 comes to my mind: "For my iniquities have gone over my head; like a heavy burden, they are too heavy for me." Each day we start fresh by asking our dear heavenly Father to lead us not into temptation but to deliver us from evil. It is only by God's grace in Christ that we can ask Him to wage war against our enemies—Satan, the world, and our own sinful flesh.

No matter what our position or situation in life, we know

that in asking for God's help and healing, we will never be alone. By admitting and confessing our personal oppressors and enemies, we will begin the salutary process of releasing and being freed from all the repressed junk in our lives, seeking God's power for the strength and ability to remove the anger, hurts, and fears caused by the enemies that plague us each and every day. By following Jesus' example of forgiveness—not only for our enemies but also for ourselves—we find peace of mind and joy in our hearts. "For it is God who works in you, both to will and to work for His good pleasure" (Philippians 2:13).

Prayer: O Lord, thank You for doing battle with our enemies, seen and unseen, throughout our journey in this life. What peace and assurance You give us each time we bow our head to pray "And lead us not into temptation, but deliver us from evil." Hear our prayer for Jesus' sake. **Amen.**

The real harm that enemies do! Fear, resentment, cynicism, lack of trust, focus on the enemy instead of God

Terry

tuesday

Personal Study Questions
Psalm 7:6–7

1. In verse 6, the psalmist urges the Lord to wake up. This plea is not uncommon in the psalms or in other places in the Old Testament. (See, for example, Psalm 35:23; 44:23; and Isaiah 51:9.)

   a. Why do you suppose so many of God's people are sometimes tempted to believe that the Lord has "fallen asleep at the switch" just when they need His help and deliverance most? *Things don't happen the way we think they should.*

   b. When have you been tempted to believe that too? *When something very evil seem happens; when lian kids become addicted, commit crimes, etc.*

2. Recall a time when a challenge created great anguish in your heart and when God did not answer your prayers right away. How did He fulfill His promise to work for good for you (Romans 8:28), despite the fact that He seemed to be sleeping?

3. How can that recollection and David's words in verses 6–7 stir hope in your heart as you consider a challenging situation in your life right now, one in which you feel powerless to fight the enemies you face?

   I'm reminded that God is in control, he does care, is involved, will bring good.

Terry

Psalm 7:8–11

*The LORD judges the peoples; judge me, O LORD,
according to my righteousness and according to the integrity
that is in me. Oh, let the evil of the wicked come to an
end, and may You establish the righteous—You who test
the minds and hearts, O righteous God! My shield is with
God, who saves the upright in heart. God is a righteous
judge, and a God who feels indignation every day.*

Leading a Double Life

Early in the morning, I love to go outside and grab the newspaper, savor the fresh air, and pause to thank God for another day of life and health in His world. Yet, many times after sitting down with my coffee and opening the paper, I am disillusioned by the shocking headlines and articles that tell of man's inhumanity to man. When I finish reading such things, I'm thankful to shift mental gears by also reading "Family Circus" and the

Terry

160

cooking section!

We live in a world impacted by natural disasters—fierce hurricanes, drought, forest fires, floods, earthquakes. Our world is also a place of drug dealers, murderers, spouse and child abusers, and angry, bitter, rebellious people. Some days it appears Satan and the wicked people of the world are winning! Outwardly, they often look like model citizens; yet, all the while, they are using—and abusing, in many cases—their positions of leadership, trust, and integrity for the cause of evil. In our world, what we see is not necessarily what we get, because people, sinful human beings, will disappoint, fail, and hurt us. God alone can judge the people of the world. He will not allow any force of evil to take away the salvation that is ours in Jesus Christ or our home in heaven.

While conducting a women's retreat several years ago, I met a lady who recently had lost her husband. During one of the sessions, I watched her eyes fill with tears as I spoke about the guilt, the pain, and the hurt we each live with during our earthly journey. My heart went out to her; I assumed she was still grieving for her husband.

When the session was over, I visited with her and expressed my deepest sympathy. She said, "Terry, I know you are busy, but perhaps you and I could talk privately?" I replied that I would be happy for us to spend some time together. Later that evening, as we talked, she poured out her heart and soul to me. "I appreciate everybody's good intentions, but nobody really knows how I am feeling about the whole situation of the life and death of my husband. People would tell me over and over again how loving, understanding, and patient my husband was with them. Yes, my husband was an accomplished man of integrity in the community and in the church. People perceived him as a wonderful husband, father, and provider. I guess two out of three aren't too bad to endure over our years together, yet I have never really confided in anyone about my pain, my guilt, or my relationship with my husband. I lived with 'Dr. Jekyll and Mr. Hyde.' He was not a loving husband but a very controlling one. I hurt in my heart that he is gone, yet nothing compares to the pain of how our family was ma-

Terry

nipulated and verbally abused over the years. I live with the guilt of being set free and not missing him as much as people believe or expect. This past month was the first time in a very long time that I woke with peace in my heart, knowing when I laid my head down that night I could truly sleep. The truth is, for the first time in many months, I have not been belittled or criticized at least a dozen times a day for a multitude of faults, from the way I wore my hair and how I dressed, to how I kept our home and cooked the meals, ran the household and cared for our children. Nothing I did was ever good enough for him. I am far from perfect, yet in his eyes, I needed to be a woman of excellence in all aspects of my life. Without God as my shield, I could not have endured the raging abuse of insults and damaging intimacy. When it suited his needs, we would receive selective snippets of his time and love, which were given in public but rarely in private."

God doesn't belittle or criticize you, and He certainly doesn't reject or control you. He is there to help you in times of need and despair. Only God is capable of loving us with a perfect love.

We talked for hours. I knew the sudden loss of her husband still hurt, yet the fear of rejection and abuse had left their telltale scars across her heart and mind. While we laughed, cried, and prayed about her life, this woman told me she had felt moved to finally share her story. I expressed my gratitude that she had confided in me and wasn't afraid to voice these feelings of hurt, anger, and rejection by the man she had promised to love and obey "'til death do us part." To all who knew her, she had seemed happy in her marriage. I couldn't fathom having to live that kind of double life. Having to cope with the fear of not being loved and living with feelings of inadequacy must have been painful to endure.

Before we left, I prayed that God would remove from her the burden of angry thoughts and emotions against her husband and that peace would fill her heart and soul. Now that she had given to the Lord this horrible injustice done to her and her family, she felt cleansed, safe, and shielded by His love. Christ alone could give her the security, peace, and integrity that were denied to her by her controlling husband. In parting, I suggested that God had

a special plan for her to share her story with others, a story she had kept hidden for so many years. And, she has! God be praised! "After you have suffered a little while, the God of all grace, who has called you to His eternal glory in Christ, will Himself restore, confirm, strengthen, and establish you" (1 Peter 5:10–11).

Many times, injured people hurt the ones that are nearest and dearest to them. We all want love, respect, and integrity. God created us with that need. If a person doesn't feel loved, there is a very deep fear of rejection. We feel that if we are just good enough and if we just do enough, we will be loved enough and have enough worth in our lives. God doesn't belittle or criticize you, and He certainly doesn't reject or control you. He is there to help you in times of need and despair. Only God is capable of loving us with a perfect love. We read in 1 Peter 4:8: "Above all, keep loving one another earnestly, since love covers a multitude of sins." That certainly pertains to the woman in this story as she released the memories of the hurtful, cruel, and abusive times and experiences in her life. Christ is our shield and refuge. He sustains us in times of peril and pain. Knowing that our Redeemer lives and loves us gives comfort beyond measure!

Prayer: Father, it is so comforting to know You are there for us in good times and bad, happy and sad. You continue to help us ease the paralyzing pains of hurt, fear, and abuse we keep hidden from the outside world. We need never fear, for You will neither leave us nor forsake us. Thank You for keeping us secure in Your love and for cleansing us from our sins so we can enjoy another day as Your children. In Jesus' name. Amen!

Terry

Personal Study Questions
Psalm 7:8–11

1. Think about the woman at the retreat described in today's faith narrative.

   a. In what ways might you identify with her? *She has things in her life that she hides; she is struggling to forgive.*

   b. How could the petitions in verses 8–11 encourage and strengthen her? *She knows God sees all and always brings justice.*

2. In verses 8–11, the psalmist's focus seems to shift, at least in part, from the injustice he himself has experienced to the injustice in the world. When have you found your own heart grieved by rampant evil that seems to proceed unchecked in the world? *Evil against children; spreading terrorism; racism; addictions*

3. What words of hope do these verses offer as you anguish over this? *God will treat each individual perfectly – He alone knows the whole story*

4. How does it help you to know that your Lord shares your indignation at the sin and wickedness all around you (v. 11)?

It helps me not to allow myself to become complacent or to spend too much emotion/words on anger

Psalm 7:12–16

*If a man does not repent, God will whet His sword;
He has bent and readied His bow; He has prepared for him
His deadly weapons, making His arrows fiery shafts. Behold,
the wicked man conceives evil and is pregnant with mischief
and gives birth to lies. He makes a pit, digging it out, and
falls into the hole that he has made. His mischief returns upon
his own head, and on his own skull his violence descends.*

Easier Said Than Done

As I was searching in my desk for a blank recipe card to jot down the ingredients for a tasty tidbit found in a magazine, I saw an oval black rock with a crudely drawn cross on it. The rock was smooth and cool to the touch as I pressed it into my hand. I closed my eyes and remembered the days Jerry and I spent in Nigeria. One day,

I had the joy of being with a group of ladies at their LWML meeting. Many of the women had traveled many miles to come to the meeting and were most eager to hear about Jesus.

A woman who gave the devotion recounted how a missionary came to her village and told her about Jesus. "At the time, I was very afraid, yet I wanted to hear what he had to say," she said. "The pastor man placed a rock in the palm of my hand. As he spoke, I looked at that stone. The man described the cross drawn on the rock and explained that Jesus died on a cross for me to take away all the bad I had done in my life. Jesus is strong like the rock I held and would help me in times of trouble, pain, and sorrow. I needed something to hold onto, as I had lost my husband and son. Jesus has carried me through many sorrows, and I am thankful for His love. Now, each time I walk to church or my ladies' meetings, I find a rock and draw a cross on it to share with a friend. Now, friend, I want you to have this rock to take with you and know that Jesus is your rock. Please remember me and pray for me."

We can love others because God first loved us, and we can also forgive others because God first forgave us. We are no longer imprisoned by what has happened in the past that would otherwise harm or frighten us.

It was very moving to see the women in that meeting express such dedication, devotion, and love for their Savior. But I was quite unprepared for our visit to the Christian Women's Shelter. We were welcomed by an elegant, ebony-skinned woman, Milo, who conducted the tour through the very clean yet sparsely furnished home. Children and women flowed in and out of the home, some with eyes hollow with fear and worry, others with expressions of joy and hope. We were told that at any time, as many as twenty-five women lived at the shelter. When our tour concluded, we were served orange drink and cookies. When I inquired about how she had come to the shelter, Milo began her profound story.

She was to be married at the tender age of fourteen to the chief of her village. Two days before her presentation to the chief, she was beaten and raped by the chief's head councilman. If Milo had spoken of this, her sisters would have suffered the same

treatment at the hands of this evil man. Milo did not appear before the chief; instead she hid in her hut. The witch doctor came to see her and saw that something bad had happened to her. He told the frightened child "the gods" were angry. How could she do this to the chief? He said, "You are unclean. You have brought shame to your people and will be punished." Late that night, she left with only a cloth wrapped around her bruised, bleeding body. For several days, she wandered aimlessly, resting only when necessary for fear of being found and put to death. She stole food to keep from starving and clothing to cover her nakedness. An old barn provided shelter for the night as exhaustion finally overtook her.

Noises awakened her early the next morning, and the smell of cooking food heightened her awareness of her empty stomach. When women came to the barn to get their pails to milk the cows, they discovered Milo. She had accidentally found the women's shelter! The women embraced her with their healing kindness and showered her with love. She was safe. Slowly her body and heart recovered from the horrors she had experienced.

Time passed and Milo realized she was pregnant. "I did many things to get rid of this baby, but nothing worked. I felt I was truly cursed," she said. "The owner of the home shared the story of the Jesus man who died to forgive sins like hate and rape. At first, I could not fathom anyone loving me. I thought somehow I had caused the rape, that I was flawed and would be faulty for the rest of my life. But when my son was born healthy, I knew that Jesus had given both of us a new life. Jesus did love me!"

Several years later, Milo met a man from her village. She asked about the chief and the councilman. The man told her that the councilman was found out for the evil he had done to the chief and the girl he was to marry. The villagers assumed she had died. The councilman was put to death before the whole village! As Psalm 7:15 says, "He makes a pit, digging it out, and falls into the hole that he has made." The councilman who had conceived evil in his heart gave birth to his own death. Yet Milo felt she was "born again" to live a new life in Jesus. The couple who started the shelter helped her to heal and educated her in life and faith.

Terry

Milo still lives at the shelter and manages it to help others in despair. God in His grace gave this truly inspirational woman the ability to develop self-confidence and inner peace. She gently took my hand and led me to the window. Out in the yard was a young boy playing and laughing. She said, "He is my son—my new life. I did not want him, but God wanted me to have this baby and raise him to His glory. When he was born, I knew love twice—first from God and then by holding a healthy baby boy."

Before we left, the assembled group of ladies asked God to continue to use her to share her painful story and her faith so other women in the same situation might know that God loves them and sent "the Jesus man" to wash away their hurts and sins.

On the dusty, muggy, hot ride back to the mission house, I reflected on the evil that had come to Milo and how God in His tender mercy had brought her through the perils of abuse and rape and had given her a new life and peace in her heart. I could not help but think about the differences between the birth of her child and the birth of most children I know. Thankfulness flooded my heart at the gift God gave us in the birth of our children.

Now back at my desk holding that rock and looking at that blank recipe card, I reflected on the wonderful, sweet ingredients of life found in our rock, Jesus Christ. We can love others because God first loved us, and we can also forgive others because God first forgave us. We are no longer imprisoned by what has happened in the past that would otherwise harm or frighten us. Thankfully, we can say, "Forgive us our debts, as we also have forgiven our debtors" (Matthew 6:12). Like Milo, we know "the Jesus man" loves us.

Prayer: Dear Jesus, thank You for Your free gift of love and grace. Help me to forgive those who have hurt and injured me by word or deed. I know You listen and heal my broken spirit and show me a new life in You. I pray this in Your name. **Amen.**

Terry

thursday

Personal Study Questions
Psalm 7:12–16

1. These verses describe the fate of the wicked, those who do not have a faith relationship with God, available by grace. Summarize their end. *They are destroyed by their own sins.*

2. In what ways do the stories in today's faith narrative illustrate the truth of these verses? *They show God's justice even on Earth- not always the case ?!*

3. Verse 12 hints at the only escape from judgment. What is it? *Repentance*

4. In kindness, God leads us to repentance (Romans 2:4). As you consider that kindness, of what sins will you repent today, relying on His mercy in Jesus?

   Non- pc. thoughts?
   Judgmental?
   Fear of others' opinions

Psalm 7:17

*I will give to the LORD the thanks
due to His righteousness, and I will sing praise
to the name of the LORD, the Most High.*

Jesus Loves Me, This I Know

When Psalm 7 was assigned to me for this portion of *A New Song,* I struggled mightily with it. Feelings I had hidden away for years tugged at my heart, and this psalm brought them all home to me. Psalm 7 is not one of joyful celebration or comfort for the soul. Rather, in these verses, David pleads with God to save and protect him from

Terry

170

his enemies and all the hurtful things in his life.

Perhaps you have experienced anger, rage, or hateful thoughts toward people who have tried to destroy or defame you or your loved ones. There was a time when I struggled with many of these same thoughts. It was truly a very painful experience as I endured stress, sleepless nights, and pain because of a few people who wounded, stabbed, and tore out chunks of my heart. At the time, the fruits of the Spirit were beyond my reach! These few people were being "joy suckers"! I was literally losing my joy and peace. Why would God allow this to happen to me and my family?

It seems God was permitting this suffering to test my compassion for the people who were causing the pain I was experiencing. And test He did! Finally, by His grace and power, I decided that bitterness and resentment were not going to be my best friends, but love and forgiveness would be. I would not continue to be a victim but a victor through the love of Christ. I prayed that God would give me an attitude of faith and graciousness so the "few" would *never* rob me of my joy in the Lord. "I sought the LORD, and He answered me and delivered me from all my fears" (Psalm 34:4). What freedom I felt when I released my problems to the Lord and changed my attitude about the situation! My burden was lifted, and the people in question have no control over me or my family.

We make choices each day regarding our attitudes. It isn't easy, but we do well to let go of ill will toward those who upset us and do wrong against us and, instead, focus on the joyful and memorable things. We certainly cannot change what hurt us in our past, nor can we change how others conduct themselves. However, we can change our attitude and how we respond to them. Only then can we recall how we have been truly blessed by God and let go of yesterday's adverse situations that paralyze us in fear and frustration.

Many years ago, a little girl went through a series of rapid challenges and changes. She experienced the pain and loneliness of abandonment, the loss of those near and dear to her, and the anxiety of a future without those special people in her life. Her

Terry

father had left home, and now she and her mother were a family of two. She struggled with questions: "When is my father coming back?" "Doesn't he care about me anymore?" "If I had been a better child, would my parents still be married?" Within two years, both of her beloved grandmothers, who had greatly influenced her life, died. Then her mother remarried, and she had a new daddy and a different last name.

At the tender age of seven, life had changed dramatically for this little girl. Fear and anxiety filled her heart as she thought about the beginning of the school year. She wanted to stay home to avoid any questions about her new life and new name. But on the appointed day for her to go into second grade at the Lutheran school, she timidly approached the classroom. Would she be welcomed? Would she belong just as before? Would Judy still be her best friend? Today it is not unusual for children of divorced parents to be students in parochial schools. However, at that time, there were no other children of divorced parents in this little girl's class, and the subject of divorce was never discussed.

Things happen for reasons that are hard for us to understand at the time; yet, how thankful we are that God in His mercy has shaped, formed, and molded us into the people we are today.

The teacher stood at the brightly decorated classroom door to greet and meet the students as they arrived. Her warm smile was very welcoming to the frightened little girl. The child whose last name had changed was afraid of not being accepted and of being teased by her classmates. She said hello to the teacher and informed her that she now had a new name and a new daddy. The teacher replied, "Oh, really? I would like to meet your new daddy. He must love you and your mother very much."

The teacher lovingly called the little girl by her new last name and directed her to her seat. As they walked hand in hand, the teacher assured the girl that Jesus loved her no matter what last name she had now. She was His special child, and Jesus would never forget her name. So, with a hug from the teacher and newfound courage, the little girl took her place in the classroom and began her first day in second grade with the confidence that

Terry

she was welcomed and accepted—and that Judy was still her best friend. After all, Jesus was trustworthy and loving, and He would take care of her for the rest of her days. "I am with you always" (Matthew 28:20).

Reassured, and with the humble awareness of the love and acceptance of her Lord, she would not focus on the old wounds of being a child of divorce and the painful memories of losing two loving, wonderful grandmothers. Instead, she would focus on a God who never left her during those dark days, on her faith in Jesus, on the lessons she learned at church and school, and on a father, a mother, and a new daddy, all of whom loved and cared for her. She looked to Jesus to heal her broken, bruised, and battered heart, asking Him to replace the pain inside with joy and happiness.

Perhaps you, too, have experienced stormy setbacks and horrendous circumstances that brought you down and held you back. Trials and tribulations are the tools by which the Lord prepares us to face bigger challenges and to be both recipients and dispensers of greater blessings in life. All the while, God is at work, giving us the ability to survive and heal as we move forward in our daily lives. Things happen for reasons that are hard for us to understand at the time; yet, how thankful we are that God in His mercy has shaped, formed, and molded us into the people we are today. His love for us is like a huge treasure chest filled with the jewels of hope, joy, and love just waiting for us to open and experience through Christ. Once we have opened that treasure chest, we are compelled by the love of Christ to share with others His unfaltering love and compassionate care.

As painful as it has been to write this devotion, I truly believe this psalm was given to me for a specific and special purpose. I believe God led me to tell about the pain and anxiety I endured as a small child going to parochial school and face the feelings that my whole world had been torn apart by my parents' divorce. I struggled with hurt feelings as I tried to understand the situation. Yet I found refuge in my heavenly Father, my mother, my friends, my teachers, and my pastor. "The truth will set you free" (John 8:32).

Terry

Knowing and trusting that God would hear my prayers and that He would rage against my enemies of loss, hurt, and anxiety, I could face each day set free by Jesus. Prayer is a powerful passion and an integral part of my daily life. Because of what happened when I was young, I have a great compassion and love for others and the trials and troubles they struggle with. Daily I reflect on God's goodness. Continually I am amazed at how He reveals Himself in my life. Psalm 23:3 speaks to me when it says: "He restores my soul. He leads me in paths of righteousness for His name's sake." I praise God for the faith that sustains me, for the family members who surround me, and for the friends who support me. I am assured, without a shadow of doubt, that "Jesus loves me! This I know, For the Bible tells me so" *(LSB* 588).

Prayer: Dear heavenly Father, You know me so well! Thank You for never leaving me and always loving me. I humbly offer my heart's gratitude in allowing me the privilege, through my pain, to minister to others who are hurting. Lord, continue to make me sensitive to Your leading, and supply me with what I need to make a difference today. I pray in Jesus' name. **Amen.**

Terry

Friday

Personal Study Questions
Psalm 7:17

1. Contrast the psalmist's mood as the psalm begins and ends.

2. While the psalmist's feelings change as the psalm progresses, what remains constant?

3. How does today's faith narrative illustrate the trustworthiness of God in the author's life? When have you experienced that same trustworthiness?

4. Evil still infects the world. No doubt, David's enemies still tell lies about him and continue to plot his demise. How, then, can he offer the thanks and praise of verse 17? How can we?

panicked, frantic

1. He's very anxious, riled at first. At the end he's peaceful, calm, having put it all back in the proper perspective.

2. He talks to God about all of it always acknowledging God's control.

3. Insomnia; forgiveness & peace of mind; presence & comfort in trouble; insight into my own feelings & faults without condemnation

4. We know the ultimate end of the story, and that here & now we have what really counts, which is untouched by human evil.

Group Bible Study for Week 5
Psalm 7

1. What new insights or key thoughts came to mind this past week as you read the faith narratives and meditated on the words of Psalm 7? How has God's Word shaped and changed you this week? *Made me aware of which "enemies" have too much power in my life.*

p. 158
Read enemies!
enemies!

2. Suppose you were to outline this psalm and give each section a title. How would you divide it? What title and subtitles would you use? Explain your reasoning.

3. As the psalm begins, David cries out to the Lord in near despair over his pursuers.

   a. In what ways does 2 Samuel 16:5–8, the probable context in which David first prayed this prayer, help to explain the depth of his anguish?

   b. Read the story's conclusion from 2 Samuel 16:9–14 and 2 Samuel 19:16–21. When God restores the kingdom to David, David shows mercy to his enemies rather than taking revenge. If David hates injustice so much, why does he allow Shimei to go unpunished?

   c. Now read 1 Kings 2:8–9, the Scripture's final footnote on Shimei's fate. To what do you attribute David's apparent change of heart and mind in his charge to Solomon? Keep in mind the command in Exodus 22:28 as you answer.

   d. So what? What insights can you derive from this for your own concerns about injustice today?

4. In verse 2, David compares his enemies to a lion.

a. What damage does this lion do?

b. This description could not possibly fit the damage an earthly animal known to zookeepers and biologists as *panthera leo* could inflict. To what or whom, then, might this verse refer? (See 1 Peter 5:8–9.)

c. Facing this "lion's" teeth, its roar, the psalmist turns to the Lord, his God, for refuge. When have you done this same thing for the same reasons? Tell about the outcome.

5. In verse 6, the psalmist seems to shout at the top of his lungs, hoping to awaken God, his Savior. "Awake for me," he prays. What comfort might the truths of Psalm 121:3–4 bring you when you feel that God has "gone to sleep" on your concerns?

6. Read verse 8 aloud. Is the psalmist arrogant (thinking he has no sin), foolish (thinking God does not know about his sin), or something else as he asks God to judge him "according to my righteousness"? Explain.

7. Psalm 7 ends on a high note of praise. How can this be, in light of all the turmoil, evil schemes, and frustration the psalmist has described in the preceding sixteen verses?

8. How did this week's faith narratives help you better understand and apply the words of Psalm 7 to your own life as God's repentant, redeemed daughter?

Week Six

Psalm 10

¹ Why, O LORD, do You stand far away?
Why do You hide Yourself in times of trouble?

² In arrogance the wicked hotly pursue the poor;
let them be caught in the schemes that they have devised.

³ For the wicked boasts of the desires of his soul,
and the one greedy for gain curses and renounces the LORD.

⁴ In the pride of his face the wicked does not seek Him;
all his thoughts are, "There is no God."

⁵ His ways prosper at all times;
Your judgments are on high, out of his sight;
as for all his foes, he puffs at them.

⁶ He says in his heart, "I shall not be moved;
throughout all generations I shall not meet adversity."

⁷ His mouth is filled with cursing and deceit and oppression;
under his tongue are mischief and iniquity.

⁸ He sits in ambush in the villages;
in hiding places he murders the innocent.
His eyes stealthily watch for the helpless;

⁹ he lurks in ambush like a lion in his thicket;
he lurks that he may seize the poor;
he seizes the poor when he draws him into his net.

¹⁰ The helpless are crushed, sink down,
and fall by his might.

¹¹ He says in his heart, "God has forgotten,
He has hidden His face, He will never see it."

¹² Arise, O Lord; O God, lift up Your hand;
forget not the afflicted.

¹³ Why does the wicked renounce God
and say in his heart, "You will not call to account"?

¹⁴ But You do see, for You note mischief and vexation,
that You may take it into Your hands;
to You the helpless commits himself;
You have been the helper of the fatherless.

¹⁵ Break the arm of the wicked and evildoer;
call his wickedness to account till You find none.

¹⁶ The Lord is king forever and ever;
the nations perish from His land.

¹⁷ O Lord, You hear the desire of the afflicted;
You will strengthen their heart; You will incline Your ear

¹⁸ to do justice to the fatherless and the oppressed,
so that man who is of the earth may strike terror no more.

Cynda Strong

Psalm 10:1

*Why, O Lord, do You stand far away? Why do
You hide Yourself in times of trouble?*

Never Alone

When I was pregnant with our first child and only a few weeks from delivery, I awoke around midnight one night to find my husband not at home. He was attending a meeting at church, and I had dozed off while waiting for him. I couldn't imagine how the meeting could still be going on, but I had no way to contact him—this was years before cell

phones. I began to panic. What if I went into labor? Our neighbors were elderly and didn't drive. My husband had our only car. The hospital was half an hour away. I was alone and had no way to contact the person I relied on the most. How could he leave me like this—by myself and helpless?

Then I thought of another frightening possibility: he'd been in an accident. I called the police and, fortunately, the officer was familiar with our vehicle, the only pumpkin-orange car in town! The officer assured me it would take only a few minutes to track my husband down. Twenty minutes later, my husband was home. Unaware of my distress and thinking I was asleep, he had refrained from calling me while he assisted a parishioner in need. He hadn't abandoned me, of course. But you couldn't have convinced me of that as I paced the floor in a panic!

Suffering alone is painful. The psalmist expresses this in the first verse of Psalm 10 when he cries out to God. It appears that God is hiding far off and is unconcerned about his problems. When we experience stress and anguish, we, too, can feel like God is far away and unaware of our concerns. When we want deliverance from our problems and don't experience immediate relief, like David, we can feel that God is not only absent, He is actully hiding from us.

When Christ hung on the cross, suffering and dying under the weight of our sins, He also knew the pain of suffering alone. Most of His disciples had fled; during His last hours, only a few remained. Even some of His most faithful followers—His women disciples—stood off at a distance. He cried out to His Father and asked why He had been forsaken (Matthew 27:46). Christ's agony—physical, mental, emotional, and spiritual—was more than we can ever imagine.

Sometimes we feel alone in our suffering when actually we are not. My husband was only blocks away when I panicked about his absence. During such times, God usually provides comfort and security through other people. Spouses, friends, co-workers, and even police officers, lift us up and encourage us. We rely on them for support, comfort, and security. But when we lack adquate sys-

Cynda

tems of support, we can begin to believe that we must face our circumstances all by ourselves. That feeling can be devastating.

In Psalm 10, David laments against the attacks of sinful men against him. These wicked oppressors are all around him doing their wicked deeds. In the midst of his suffering, David reacted as we all do. The emotions he experienced were human. He felt like no one was there to help him, that even God had abandoned him. But those times are times when we need to cry out to God like David did. Those are times when we should consider that God has a plan for us and He will work out all things for our good (Romans 8:28).

As I write this, is hasn't rained in my area for nearly six weeks. Everyone wants rain! But just a few months ago, we wanted relief from storms that came every day. This teaches me that if things are always the way we want them, or we are always in our comfort zone, we may see no reason to turn to God for His help and strength.

God uses our feelings of loneliness and helplessness to cause us to examine ourselves and reevaluate our lives. Is there something He wants to teach me through His Word? Is there a sin that I have avoided to confess? Has He turned away from me, or have I turned away from Him? Is He hiding from me, or am I hiding a part of my life from Him? How can I come back into His presence and feel the comfort and security I long for?

It is then that our emotions serve His purpose. Through His Word, God opens our eyes to all that we were missing. We repent of our sins, of not following His will, and we recall His promises made to us in Christ. Jesus promised that He will never leave or forsake us. In desperate times, we rely on His promise and hold fast to it. His Spirit dwells within our hearts. When we feel alone, even with no earthly help in sight, we can focus on God and His Word. The promises in His Word are stronger than our emotions that sometimes can make us feel like no one cares.

I never realized how much I had in common with Old Testament heroes. Their lives appeared so far removed from mine, their problems so different. Heroes like Moses had a rough

Cynda

existence. Every time he tried to follow God, he ran into what appeared to be insurmountable opposition. But Moses remained a strong and faithful leader and example. In Deuteronomy 31:6, Moses talks to God's people. No doubt they feared the difficulties yet to come. Yet Moses assured them that God would remain faithful: "Be strong and courageous. Do not fear or be in dread of them, for it is the LORD your God who goes with you. He will not leave you or forsake you." A few chapters later, God assured Joshua that He would be beside him too: "No man shall be able to stand before you all the days of your life. Just as I was with Moses, so I will be with you. I will not leave you or forsake you" (Joshua 1:5).

As great leaders set apart by God, David, Moses, and Joshua were faced with situations most of us will never endure. An entire nation depended on their strength and faith. Surely they felt alone in coping with huge burdens and doubts. But God kept His promises and lifted them up and provided for their needs.

But what God promised them, God now promises you. "I will never leave you nor forsake you" (Deuteronomy 31:6; Hebrews 13:5). We give thanks to God for giving us people to help and support us. But our eternal help is in God. He will never leave us. Through Christ's Word and Sacraments, He draws us closer to Himself. His death and resurrection sealed our eternal relationship with Him. We need never feel alone nor abandoned. For those who are lonely or afraid, Jesus promises, "I am with you always, to the end of the age" (Matthew 28:20).

Prayer: Dear God, when I feel alone, I long for Your comfort to make me feel secure. Thank You for allowing me to see that when these times come, I can turn to You in Your Word. Your Holy Spirit dwells within me and Your holy angels attend me. Thank You that You will never leave me. In Jesus' name. **Amen.**

Cynda

monday

Personal Study Questions
Psalm 10:1

1. Many of the psalms we have been studying have included sentiments like those of Psalm 10:1. Have the words or the intensity of the psalmist's emotions surprised or even shocked you? Explain.

2. The Holy Spirit not only inspired these psalms, He also has seen to it that the psalms were preserved for us through the centuries so we can pray them today. How does remembering that help you?

3. Psalm 10 begins on a note of frustration and irritability that borders on anger. It's as though the psalmist (possibly David) has stalked into God's throne room to dump his concern on the table and vent his ire.

   a. What two questions does he blurt out?

   b. Do you see these questions as disrespectful? Explain.

   c. What might spur you to ask the same questions as the psalmist?

4. The psalmist uses God's personal name throughout this psalm. That name, LORD, is often translated "Yahweh" or "Jehovah." God revealed it to Moses at the burning bush. This reminds the reader of the Lord's covenant-making, covenant-keeping character. (See Exodus 3:13–17.)

   a. How does this help you read the words as faith-filled and heart-felt?

   b. How does remembering your baptismal covenant help you pray the words in confident hope?

Psalm 10:2–7

In arrogance the wicked hotly pursue the poor; let them
be caught in the schemes that they have devised. For
the wicked boasts of the desires of his soul, and the one
greedy for gain curses and renounces the LORD.

Let Them
Be Caught

It was painful then; now, more than twenty years later, it's still a dull ache. David writes how the wicked hotly pursue the poor, or any other victim for that matter. The wicked use whatever means necessary to reach their goal, whether power, revenge, or just the enjoyment of other people's suffering. Unfortunately, the incident I am about to share with you occurred within a congregation. Sadly, it was perpetuated by some church members on other members and upon the pastor, my husband.

Our church body had just released a new hymnal. Several members of our congregation had grown up with the "old" hymnal and were determined that the new one would never find a home in our congregation. True, there were differences in the hymnals. But for these few people, different words and tunes were enough for them to reject the new hymnal outright.

We may suffer awhile for now, but with God's help, we can turn away from bitterness, anger, and hurt, and know that the Lord will act on our behalf.

Although our pastor, organist, and choir worked hard to introduce the new services and songs to our members, nothing seemed to appease these folks. The new services were explained and practiced; still, unhappy people seemed determined to keep the new hymnal out of the congregation. Ultimately, they resorted to trickery, gossip, and lies. Soon my husband was receiving seething correspondence, was rudely treated at meetings, and was even falsely accused of all sorts of things in the city's Sunday newspaper. Most congregational members saw the situation for what it was—evil in action. Those days are now past; we refer to them as the "Great Hymnal War." Thanks be to God, when our congregation recently adopted our church body's newest hymnal, it was by unanimous vote, with barely any discussion.

In the verses for today, the psalmist describes evil in action. Almost anyone can identify with situations like this. A clear example today is terrorism; destruction by terrorists is not limited to method, place, or target. Closer to home, we may know someone whose actions can be identified as evil. It may be someone in the workplace, school, even the Church. And their actions can frighten us! As David writes, "In arrogance the wicked hotly pursue the poor" (v. 2). The wicked deny God's power and take pride in their own. They use people for their own purpose, even if that purpose is simply to see others suffer. In this psalm we are shown that an evil person may be deceitful and even pretend to worship God, but he is greedy and rejects all that God really is and what He wants. The evil person believes that since God does not strike out at him, he can continue in his evil ways (v. 4). Perhaps God will

Cynda

never find him out, he imagines. In his arrogance, he continues to devour, greedy for more control and power. As God remains silent, he grows in arrogance and soon feels above God and other people (v. 5). He thinks that no one can harm him.

Such a person is so confident that he sees himself victorious over everyone he encounters, especially the weak and defenseless. He relies totally on himself. All his actions exemplify all that we as humans consider evil. He speaks with deceit and violence. He injures anyone he wants and takes great pleasure in doing so. Who would want to be in the presence of such a person? You would not escape his presence unscathed. You could not trust his motives. You would have to protect yourself in case he turned on you at any moment.

While we readily see the evil in others and feel the result of their attacks, it is harder to accept that we, too, think evil thoughts and act in evil ways. Each of us is born with original sin and commits evil acts daily. Apart from the Holy Spirit, we are incapable of doing good. Our hearts and minds constantly draw us toward prideful endeavors. We seek fame, prestige, and recognition to feel better about ourselves and worse about others. By doing so, we say to ourselves and to God that we are more important than He. We seek what benefits us, not what benefits our neighbor. In the process, we ignore the helpless, the weak, and the needy. We forget God and all He hopes for us. Our arrogance nurses injuries and old wounds; we bemoan our misfortunes and wonder at those whose blatant evil actions go unchecked.

When we suffer evil directed against us, we go to the cross. But where do we go when we finally admit that we have committed evil against others? Again, we go to the cross. In the broken body and poured-out blood of our Savior, we find relief. There, on Calvary, Jesus faced evil head-on—and suffered for it. But while evil appeared victorious, through Jesus' sufferings and death, evil was defeated. Forever. In Jesus' wounds we find healing for the scars left by the wicked words and deeds of other people. In His wounds we also find forgiveness for our evil thoughts, words, and deeds. And in the bright rays of His glorious resurrection, we see

Cynda

the light of own eternal home and the final judgment against the wicked. The wicked deny God and never repent. In their unbelief, they harm His precious children. We may suffer awhile for now, but with God's help, we can turn away from bitterness, anger, and hurt, and know that the Lord will act on our behalf against the wicked. With David, we can pray, "Let [the wicked] be caught in the schemes that they have devised" (v. 2).

The Great Hymnal War left those who were wounded in spirit on both sides of the battlefield. My husband was spiritually injured and physically weakened. And while scars are still felt today, we are still drawn to the precious wounds of Christ. And we've experienced God's abundant and undeserved blessings. Our newest hymnal was adopted without strife. Many new members in our church family have no knowledge of past hurts and disagreements. And while those who do remember are keenly aware of the devil's evil ways, God is still ministering to their spirits.

Because Jesus met evil head-on for us and won, we can follow the words of St. Paul: "Beloved, never avenge yourselves, but leave it to the wrath of God, for it is written, 'Vengeance is mine, I will repay, says the Lord.' To the contrary, 'if your enemy is hungry, feed him; if he is thirsty, give him something to drink; for by so doing you will heap burning coals on his head.' Do not be overcome by evil, but overcome evil with good" (Romans 12:19–21).

Prayer: Lord God, sometimes we are weak and fall victim to the weakness of our sinful human nature and the evil ways of the devil. Send Your Holy Spirit to remind us of the peace and safety that come only from You. Lead us to repentance. Forgive us our sins, and help us to forgive others. For Jesus' sake. Amen.

Cynda

tuesday

Personal Study Questions
Psalm 10:2–7

1. When have you experienced hurt because of the actions of evil people? When have your own actions qualified as evil? Explain.

2. As in other psalms we have studied in this volume, Psalm 10 details the behavior of the wicked. What behaviors and attitudes do you note in Psalm 10 that you have not seen in the psalms we studied earlier?

3. In what ways do these behaviors and attitudes fit the human enemies of God's people today? What does this tell you about human nature?

4. Despite the rebellion of the wicked, "his ways prosper at all times" (v. 5). How does this prosperity contrast with the true prosperity—forgiveness, life, and peace—God has given you in His Son, Jesus?

2. - Very deliberate plotting against the poor innocent weak;
   - Conscious arrogance toward God - Believes God is not there
   - Thinks no one will oppose him

3. Same! "There's nothing new under the sun"

4. I don't make them happen; they are permanent, guaranteed, and genuine!

Cynda

Psalm 10:8–11

He sits in ambush in the villages; in hiding places
he murders the innocent. His eyes stealthily watch for the
helpless; he lurks in ambush like a lion in his thicket.

A Lion
By Your Side

In a way, bullies are like lions.

Think about it. Bullies lurk on school playgrounds and in classrooms, in cubicles and in board rooms. They inflict emotional if not physical pain. They concentrate their efforts on the weak and powerless. They don't seem to care about their actions. Perhaps you have witnessed someone enduring either painful physical blows or cruel, verbal assaults at the hand or mouth of a bully. Bullying can even go on at

Cynda

190

home. Psychologists tell us that bullies intentionally terrorize others to gain power and recognition. Like a lion whose "eyes stealthily watch for the helpless" (v. 8), a bully can master the art of subtle intimidation and behavior meant to demean and frighten. What is most alarming is that bullies can perfect this behavior so that it goes undetected.

With more than twenty-five years of teaching experience, I've seen my share of both overt and covert bullying among young people. For example, one year, the senior class at our school included several girls who were beautiful in the light but vicious and conniving in the shadows. They formed two rival cliques and proceeded to make one another's lives miserable. No hallway, locker area, classroom, or social event escaped their warfare. Insults and gossip were their weapons of choice, and they used them to injure the reputations of others.

Although the rivalry lasted throughout the year, savvy faculty held it in check. Parents were advised of blatant offenses, students and parents talked together, and counselors talked to the students with compassion and a focus on God's Word. Today, these young women have matured and no longer resemble the bullies in the hallways. But it is unlikely that they have completely forgotten the battles or have escaped without some emotional scars.

The effects of bullying can leave permanent damage. Bullied children may assume aggressive behavior themselves or withdraw from relationships with others. As these victims grow into adulthood, sometimes they never have the opportunity or means to heal. Victims are found in the home, workplace, and even in church. Like lions, bullies aren't particular about their target, yet they tend to attack the weak. Like the lion in today's psalm, the bully believes, "God has forgotten. . . . He will never see it." It's because of this devil-may-care attitude and the emotional scars it leaves on its victims that bullying must be addressed.

Today, the psalmist introduces us to another bully—in this case, David's enemy—who delights in the weakness of his victims. Like a lion, this bully lurks "in hiding places" and lies "in ambush." Cunning yet cowardly, "his eyes stealthily watch" for a

Any abuse of power – teachers who humiliate; bosses who yell...

Cynda

191

victim. He "seizes the poor," and "the helpless are crushed." Such words show the bully's sneaky, calculating means of attack—all well thought out with the goal of inflicting pain and suffering. In verse 8 the bully murders, and in verse 9 he draws another victim into his net. And who falls prey to his plotting and scheming? The innocent, the helpless, the poor—all those without the strength or means to defeat him.

Jesus is always ready to aid the poor and helpless. When we are bullied or feel that we're being torn apart by lions, God always provides assistance.

The lion is used as a metaphor for bullies in other places in Scripture. King Solomon warns, "Like a roaring lion or a charging bear is a wicked ruler over a poor people" (Proverbs 28:15). The prophet Isaiah says of the wicked, "Their roaring is like a lion, like young lions they roar; they growl and seize their prey; they carry it off, and none can rescue" (Isaiah 5:29). The prophet Ezekiel says of false prophets, "The conspiracy of her prophets in her midst is like a roaring lion tearing the prey; they have devoured human lives; they have taken treasure and precious things; they have made many widows in her midst" (Ezekiel 22:25). There are other similar passages.

Of course, the ultimate bully is our archenemy, Satan. Peter refers to Satan as a lion when he admonishes us, "Be sober-minded; be watchful. Your adversary the devil prowls around like a roaring lion, seeking someone to devour" (1 Peter 5:8). Satan seeks to consume our eternal souls. To help him do that, he stands behind every bully in our lives, tempting them to focus on their pain and inadequacies and to seek relief through hurting us with their words or deeds. But like the cheap fix of an illegal drug, the relief doesn't last. So the bully keeps on bullying.

Satan, the roaring lion who seeks to devour us, met his match, of course, in the Lion of the tribe of Judah (Revelation 5:5). This Lion has conquered our enemies of sin, death, and hell. But unlike the typical bully, this Lion did not come to hurt or harm; He came to suffer and die. And He did so by becoming the Lamb (v. 8) who was slain on the altar of the cross. His blood ransomed us for God and made us "a kingdom and priests to our God" (v. 10). Indeed, in perhaps the world's greatest irony, our mighty and

all-powerful Lion, our Savior, Jesus Christ, is the meek and lowly "Lamb of God, who takes away the sin of the world" (John 1:29).

In Psalm 10:8–10, things are at their darkest, the writer is at his lowest, and his situation seems hopeless. We may have similar feelings about the place or state we're in. But we know that our Savior has valiantly fought and won the battle against the ultimate bully. The ultimate victor, Jesus, is always ready to aid the poor and helpless. When we are bullied or feel that we're being torn apart by lions, God always provides assistance.

Who are your bullies? With Christ by your side, you can fight against them and be freed from their control. Our archbully, the devil, has already lost. In truth, this murdering and lying lion has been defanged and declawed and now purrs like a harmless kitten. Through Christ's sacrificial death and glorious resurrection, we have the victory.

So, don't be afraid. Meet your bullies head on! Standing beside you is the most gracious and most powerful Lion in the universe. May Jesus be praised!

Prayer: We are weak, Lord, and You are strong. Help us to recognize when others need us. Equip us and guide us so we can stand up to the bullies in this world. And remind us daily that You will never leave us or forsake us. In Jesus' name. **Amen.**

Cynda

wednesday

Personal Study Questions
Psalm 10:8–11

1. In verse 4, the wicked espouse flagrant atheism ("There is no God"). In verse 11, God's enemies express what some have called "practical atheism" ("God has forgotten, He has hidden His face, He will never see it"). Such practical atheism supports a lifestyle lived as though the Lord, His Law, and His love do not matter— whether they exist or not.

   a. When have you lived as though God's will for you was irrelevant? *Every day! In moments when I feel in charge, when it feels good to indulge my own whims — eating, time-wasting*

   b. What will you say to Him about that now? *Guide me! change me! I'm sorry!*

2. Sin deceives those who practice it.

   a. Find three lies from verses 4–11 that the wicked tell themselves. How do these lies create bullying behavior as described in today's faith narrative?

   b. Do you know people who believe lies like these today? Explain how that self-deception can happen.

a. There is no God; I'll never be opposed; God has forgotten — sense of power; evil sense of freedom that leads to total self-indulgence slavery to evil impulses!

b. In any particular area of our lives where we don't acknowledge God's LORDSHIP — Wall Street investors; ~~Anti state~~ papparazzi; marital cheats; scam artists; vicious tongues

Psalm 10:12–15

Arise, O LORD; O God, lift up Your hand; forget not the afflicted. Why does the wicked renounce God and say in his heart, "You will not call to account"?

The Best-Laid Plans

I'm a long-range planner, especially when it comes to vacations. I love to plot the course, identify sites along the way, and reserve the lodgings. I find coupons, use frequent-flier miles, and buy tickets well in advance. Planning is my safety net—I don't want to drive around a strange city looking for a vacancy sign, or miss anything exciting.

But sometimes planning can become confining. When

195

we must be in a certain location by a certain time, we miss the chance for spontaneity along the way. A side-road adventure or grabbing an ice-cream cone might interfere with getting somewhere on time.

I remind myself of this nearly every time I travel. My most memorable trip was traveling through the English countryside with a good friend. We had carefully planned our route from one bed-and-breakfast to the next. As a reader of Elizabethan history, I had plotted the course to visit sites related to the reign of Elizabeth I, while my friend had marked all the National Trust gardens. Between us, we would navigate sixteenth-century history and the beautiful countryside. But while traveling to one of our destinations, we passed a sign indicating public admittance to an English home nearby. It was not on our schedule, and we had no knowledge of its significance, but we had time, so we took the turn. The "home" was the 1,400-acre estate of Queen Elizabeth's chief of state, William Cecil, Lord Burghley. Touring this home full of Elizabethan treasures and surrounded by magnificent gardens became the highlight of the trip—an unplanned find.

In this life, we may never know the reason for our suffering or the scope of His plan, but we take comfort in the fact that He promises never to leave us. Life's detours will bring the blessing of drawing us closer to Him.

God has plans for each of us (Jeremiah 29:11–13). Those plans are always for our good, never for our harm. Through faith in Christ, we have a personal relationship with God our heavenly Father, who reconciled us to Himself through His Son. But what do we do when it appears like wickedness is winning, like David must have felt when he wrote Psalm 10? It is hard to comprehend that God is acting according to His plan for our lives when bad things happen to us—and to others. Surely He could stop war, pain, sickness, death, and all other heartaches. But God has the master plan of *all* lives; His plans all work together for our good. Believing that is impossible, humanly speaking. It requires God-given faith.

When we experience stress, fear, and the weight of illness, we can feel alone in the world. The wicked deeds of others, as

[handwritten notes in margin: "Cynda me. God help me. This is the story of every point day. A VITAL TRUTH - Gives life here & eternally"]

well as financial, relationship, and health problems, can weigh us down. Too often we look to the world for assistance. We plan our finances, education, and retirement. At the same time, however, we worry that those plans are in vain. Sometimes those we love the most—spouses, relatives, friends, and neighbors—cannot help us. And yet, the psalmist points out that God always knows our needs. God says in His Word that we are His children, and we are renewed with hope. Sometimes our heavenly Father waits patiently for us to seek His ways. As He waits, He is always present, watching over us, ready to lift us up from the dangers and stresses of each day.

Psalm 10:14 calls on the victims of wickedness to commit their lives and futures to God, who will protect and comfort them, and exact justice on their enemies. As long as we are on this earth, we will never be immune to pain, difficult times, or temptation. However, even when it appears that God is hiding and wickedness is winning, we know that God has triumphed over evil, that His kingdom is eternal. Jesus' death and resurrection have assured us of that.

In Romans 8:18–25, Paul assures us that our present sufferings—be they physical, spiritual, financial, or relational—cannot be compared to what God has planned for us in eternity. Our present pain is miniscule compared to the everlasting joys we will experience in heaven. Even when we feel all is lost or that God does not seem to hear or care, verses 24 and 25 encourage us to have hope and to persevere. God allows our suffering so we are drawn more and more to the promises He makes to us in His Word. Trusting in His Word, we wait patiently for the hope we cannot even see. When we view our plight, it may seem that all is hopeless. Yet there is a light at the end of the tunnel. "And we know that for those who love God all things work together for good, for those who are called according to His purpose" (Romans 8:28).

And while we wait with patience, we rest in the knowledge that our suffering cannot separate us from God's love (v. 38). Our salvation is secure. Our life here, filled with both joy and sorrow, is temporary. Through His perfect obedience and His sufferings

Cynda

and death, Christ earned for us a better life. We wait for "our blessed hope, the appearing of the glory of our great God and Savior, Jesus Christ, who gave Himself for us to redeem us from all lawlessness and to purify for Himself a people for His own possession who are zealous for good works" (Titus 2:13–14).

As we draw closer to Christ with the knowledge of His love, we rely on Him more and more. Even when we stumble and fall, He lovingly protects us according to His plan. When life's detours put pain or stress into our lives, God is always there to guide and comfort us. In this life, we may never know the reason for suffering or the scope of His plan, but we take comfort in the fact that He will never leave us. Even life's unexpected detours can draw us closer to Him.

As we plan our days, beginning with morning prayer for God's grace and ending with bedtime prayer of thanksgiving for His blessings each hour, we know that He is faithful in keeping us in His care. Whether we stay on course, take a detour, or get lost, our triune God forgets us not.

Every

fear

A given

Cynda

Prayer: Almighty God, this earthly life is one of suffering and uncertainty—all because of sin and Satan. Only You, Lord, offer mercy and forgiveness. Only You. Grant me peace and comfort, and through Your Word and Sacraments, keep me steadfast in my faith in Your redeeming love. In Jesus' name. **Amen.**

thursday

Personal Study Questions
Psalm 10:12–15

1. Faced with all the stealth of the wicked and the apparent power of God's enemies (vv. 1–11), the psalmist might have fallen into utter despair. But verse 12 marks a turning point of sorts. How so?

2. Which statements of faith in verses 12–15 do you find especially meaningful, particularly as you think about the issues over which you personally lament today?

3. Reread these verses with your Savior's cross and open tomb front and center in your mind. How do the words fittingly describe what God has done for us in Jesus?

Psalm 10:16–18

The LORD is king forever and ever; the nations perish from His land. O LORD, You hear the desire of the afflicted; You will strengthen their heart; You will incline Your ear to do justice to the fatherless and the oppressed, so that man who is of the earth may strike terror no more.

God's Perfect Timing

My husband was finishing his year of vicarage, and we were preparing to move back to our home for his final year of seminary. We were relying on my returning to teaching for this last year. We had saved enough money for his tuition and books for the first term, but we

Cynda

needed a regular income for living expenses and the tuition, fees, and books for the following terms.

Then, only a few weeks before our move and the start of school, I was informed that no teaching position was available in the public school district. Panic set in. Here we were, only one year left, with no foreseeable income. How could God not come through for us now that we had come this far?

I made a long-distance call to the parochial high school in the town where the seminary was located, but I found no openings there either. The principal did say to check with her after our move in case something became available later. My husband assured me that God would provide, and in the meantime, he would look for a part-time job. But I was a little disappointed in God.

A few weeks later, we arrived at the seminary, quickly settled into our apartment, and my husband started classes. And just as quickly, I lined up an interview at a local radio station—a far cry from the teaching work I desired. I locked the apartment door one morning and had just started down the stairs when I heard the phone ring. Since the phone had been installed only two days earlier, it seemed unlikely that anyone would know the number.

I raced back up the stairs, unlocked the door, and breathlessly answered the phone. On the line was the principal of the parochial school. She asked if I could possibly start teaching the very next day! Sadly, one of the school's teachers had died just days before, so they had an immediate opening. I would be teaching the same grade level and using textbooks I was familiar with.

The timing still amazes me. My one-year teaching experience at this school has become a matter of family history. The next year we moved away from our seminary home, but eventually my husband was called to serve a church in that community. Renewing friendships I'd made at the school led to years of part-time teaching. My daughter is now teaching there, and my relationship with the school continues as I teach part time in the summer.

God had a plan that I couldn't see. His timing made all the difference. His timing led to blessings upon a generation yet unborn.

Cynda

In Psalm 10, the psalmist has spent much time describing the evil we must endure on this earth. He has expressed confidence that God is in charge and will triumph. He knows God hears the pleas of the helpless and will come to their aid. But if the psalmist is like me, in the back of his mind, he is also saying *"When?"* Our natural, mostly unspoken prayer to God is often "Do it now!" We want relief *now*. But patience and peace come from committing our lives into God's keeping. It's just hard to do; in fact, apart from His grace, it is impossible! It requires God's gift of faith and the Spirit's fruit of patience.

Because of Jesus' victory over death and the grave, we can rest, secure in the knowledge that whatever the outcome, God is working in all things for our good (Romans 8:28).

The psalmist assures us in verse 17 that God knows and hears our cries of need. In verse 18, he says He will defend us against all evil on earth. Earthly evil, pain, stress, and suffering are temporary. God's mercy lifts us beyond the temporal to rely on Him also for what is eternal. Throughout history, God has shown His faithfulness to those who love Him. In fact, God is so loving that He extends His care even to those who do not return His love. "He makes His sun rise on the evil and on the good, and sends rain on the just and on the unjust" (Matthew 5:45b).

If we look to Psalm 27, we see David praising the goodness of God. He expresses confidence that although he may not see God in action, he is sure of God's knowledge of the situation. The psalmist does not fear the evil that surrounds him (v. 3) for he knows that God will take care of him (v. 5). He knows also that those who speak ill of him and try to beat him down will be brought to justice (v. 12). He offers encouragement in verse 14 when he tells us to be strong and courageous as we patiently wait for God's timing.

Even confident of his deliverance, David tells us in Psalm 28 that we do need to express our needs to God. Here he calls on God to rescue him and not allow the evil, wicked enemies to destroy him. We likewise pray in the Lord's Prayer, "Deliver us from evil" (Matthew 6:13). David expresses his desire that God tear down his enemies for the evil they have done. And he confidently prais-

Cynda

es God (Psalm 28:6), knowing he has been heard. When we, like David, tell God our specific needs, we are released from our anxieties and find comfort as we commit our lives into His care. David expresses in this psalm the knowledge that God has heard his cries; in joyful response, his heart is lifted, and he offers thanks. And all this is *before* God has acted!

By our human standards, God's timing seems awfully slow. But God's timing is always perfect. We may not understand the delay. We may want answers and solutions immediately. But in prayer, we can ask our heavenly Father to come to our aid, to give us patience, to comfort and defend us, and to lift us up. We can ask other Christians for their prayers. We can offer praise through word and song, and we can read and meditate on His Word. Through the Gospel and the Sacraments, our souls are comforted and we are able to recognize more and more of God's kindness and goodness toward us. As Paul writes, "the peace of God, which surpasses all understanding, will guard [our] hearts and [our] minds in Christ Jesus" (Philippians 4:7).

Because of Jesus' victory over death and the grave, we can rest, secure in the knowledge that whatever the outcome, God is working in all things for our good (Romans 8:28). We can enjoy a lifestyle that shows our confidence in Him. Strengthened by His grace, we can consider the situations of others and look for ways to assist them and lift them out of their struggles. As we ourselves are comforted by God's tender mercy, we can comfort others (2 Corinthians 1:3–4).

Our need for problems to be solved and answers given according to our timetable simply reflects our desire for control. The sure knowledge of sins forgiven in Christ releases us from bondage to that sin. God's timing is always perfect. We see that in the incarnation and birth of His Son: "But when the fullness of time had come, God sent forth His Son, born of woman, born under the law, to redeem those who were under the law, so that we might receive adoption as sons" (Galatians 4:4–5).

So, take your troubles to God in prayer. Have confidence that because you are His precious daughter, He will indeed hear your

Bondage to committing to sin ... and to remorse, fear, self-deception ...

cry for mercy. And wait on Him. He will bless you in His own perfect time.

Prayer: Abba, Father, hear our prayer! We are anxious and impatient. Teach us to wait for You. We are uncertain and afraid. Assure us that Your love and compassion are so great that You sent Your only Son, our Lord Jesus Christ, for our salvation. Strengthen and preserve us, Lord, through Him. In Jesus' name. **Amen.**

Friday

Personal Study Questions
Psalm 10:16–18

1. Here we read a battle cry that shouts news of complete victory! Which assurances in these verses do you most need to hear and apply to yourself in faith today? Why?

2. "Man"—mere human beings who live apart from a new life in Christ—are "of the earth" (v. 18). How does remembering this help you face the challenges of your life, particularly when you remember your Savior has "raised [you] up with Him and seated [you] with Him in the heavenly places in Christ Jesus" (Ephesians 2:6)?

3. Today's faith narrative offers practical advice for us when we struggle to wait patiently for God to act on our behalf. Which of these suggestions has worked for you in the past? Which might you rely upon today?

Bible Study for Week 6
Psalm 10

1. Which faith narrative from this week seemed to speak most aptly to your personal situation right now? Explain.

2. Reflect on your overall impressions after studying Psalm 10. How would you describe it? Realistic? idealistic? pessimistic? optimistic? out-of-date? contemporary? Explain.

3. Read the psalm again, noting all the phrases that describe "the wicked" or "the evil" in each of the following categories:

   a. What the wicked/evil do

   b. What the wicked/evil say or think

   c. What outcomes the wicked/evil receive

4. To what examples in the world today can you point to demonstrate the accuracy of the descriptions you found in your answers for question 3?

5. Now read the psalm again, this time noting all the phrases that describe the "poor," the "weak," the "helpless," the "victims," the "afflicted," the "fatherless," and the "oppressed." Like the "poor," the "mourners," the "meek," the "hungry and thirsty," and the "persecuted" whom Jesus describes in the Sermon on the Mount (Matthew 5:2–11), the unfortunates listed in Psalm 10 realize their need for forgiveness, grace, and compassion from the Lord, and they look to their Savior-God to do for them what they cannot do for themselves.

a. How does Psalm 10 describe these people—God's people?

b. What outcomes do they receive?

c. How do these promises encourage you?

6. This volume of *A New Song* ties together the six psalms we have studied under the title *Save Me, O My God: Psalms of Lament.*

a. How does each of the six psalms you have studied fit appropriately under this title?

b. How has the raw honesty of these psalms encouraged you to pray more boldly or more confidently, especially in times of anger, frustration, anxiety, or dismay? Consider the psalm texts and the faith narratives based on them.

c. For what will you praise Jesus as you close your time together today? For what will you thank Him?

Small-Group Leader's Guide

This guide will help guide you in discovering the truths of God's Word. It is not exhaustive, however, nor is it designed to be read aloud during your session.

1. Before you begin, spend some time in prayer, asking God to strengthen your faith through a study of His Word. The Scriptures were written so that we might believe in Jesus Christ and have life in His name (John 20:31). Also, pray for participants by name.

2. Before your meeting, review the session material, read the Bible passages, and answer the questions in the spaces provided. Your familiarity with the session will give you confidence as you lead the group.

3. As a courtesy to participants, begin and end each session on time.

4. Have a Bible dictionary or similar resource handy to look up difficult or unfamiliar names, words, and places. Ask participants to help you in this task. Be sure that each participant has a Bible and a study guide.

5. Ask for volunteers to read introductory paragraphs and Bible passages. A simple "thank you" will encourage them to volunteer again.

6. See your role as a conversation facilitator rather than a lecturer. Don't be afraid to give participants time to answer questions. By name, thank each participant who answers; then invite other input. For example, you might say, "Thank you, Maggie. Would anyone else like to share?"

7. Now and then, summarize aloud what the group has learned by studying God's Word.

8. Remember that the questions provided are discussion starters. Allow participants to ask questions that relate to the session. However, keep discussions on track with the session.

9. Everyone is a learner! If you don't know the answer to a question, simply tell participants that you need time to look at more Scripture passages or to ask your pastor.

Week 1, Psalm 3

Personal Study Questions

Monday—Psalm 3:1–2

1. David probably refers to Absalom and the co-conspirators who followed his treasonous lead. The account of this sad series of events from 2 Samuel also describes the insults and unfaithfulness of several in Israel who had enjoyed the safety and prosperity David's government had brought and who, thus, could have been expected to help, but did not.

2. Absalom and his army acted unwittingly as agents of Satan, who, throughout the Old Testament era, tried to subvert the Lord's promise to send the Savior. For a graphic but poetic description of this, see Revelation 12:1–4; the "woman" here represents Israel.

3. David seems to feel overwhelmed. Note the repeated use of the word *many*. The number and strength of his foes seem to stun and perhaps even bewilder him in ways reminiscent of the incidents described in today's faith narrative.

4. The lie God cannot or will not help comes from Satan himself and from our sinful flesh. No matter how loudly or how often it is repeated, it is always untrue! God saved us in Jesus; sin and Satan cannot defeat us.

Tuesday—Psalm 3:3–4

1. Answers will vary.

2. Answers will vary. It likely lifts our hearts in worship to remember and contrast the number and power of our enemies (vv. 1–2) in the light of our Lord's certain love and rescue (vv. 3–4).

3. Answers will vary.

Wednesday—Psalm 3:5–6

1. Answers will vary.

2. In verses 1–2, David seems overwhelmed with the many enemies that have arisen against him, but in verse 6, his confident hope in God has returned. Now, he does not fear "many thousands."

3. Answers will vary.

Thursday—Psalm 3:7

1. Just as the Lord had delivered His people from all their enemies during their wilderness wanderings, fulfilling His promises to bring them into the land He had promised to Abraham, so He would now keep His promises to protect David and bring the Savior from his line. Echoing the refrain, David encourages himself and rallies God's people, who face difficulties of every kind.

2. God will "strike all [His] enemies on the cheek" and will "break the teeth of the wicked."

3. In His cross and open tomb, our Savior totally defeated Satan and humiliated him in his pitiful attempt to destroy us and pull us away from God's love.

4. Answers will vary.

Friday—Psalm 3:8

1. Answers will vary.
2. Answers will vary.
3. Answers will vary.

Group Bible Study

1. Answers will vary.

2. Answers will vary. Participants will likely draw evidence from the dire situation described in verses 1–2.

3. Answers will vary, but may include the idea of "the warrior God who takes my side."

4. Answers will vary.

5. Answers will vary. Let group members share insights. It appears that the psalmist began to meditate on the salvation others warned he would never see (v. 2). The promises and love of God, combined with the good night's sleep of verse 5 totally change David's focus from fear to faith. Likewise, meditation on our Savior-God's salvation—His full and free forgiveness for all our sins, won on Calvary, and His help in every time of trouble—will change our own focus in times of fear and adversity.

6. Answers will vary.

Week 2, Psalm 4

Personal Study Questions

Monday—Psalm 4:1–2

1. Several phrases describe the psalmist's distress. See especially verses 2 and 6.

2. Answers will vary.

3. Verse 1 asks God to be gracious in answering the cry of distress. Both grace and mercy come to us as undeserved gifts, flowing from the sacrifice of Jesus for our sins on Calvary's cross.

4. Answers will vary.

Tuesday—Psalm 4:3–4

1. Answers will vary.

2. The psalmist's enemies seek David's shame, dwell on lies, and worship false gods. The Lord honors His people by singling them out for His special care, hearing their prayers, and, by implication, helping them in distress. No false god could or would do any of this!

3. Answers will vary.

Wednesday—Psalm 4:5

1. Psalm 51 describes them in these words: "The sacrifices of God are a broken spirit; a broken and contrite heart, O God, You will not despise." Thus the Spirit points us to the repentance and faith He Himself gives as we humble ourselves under His mighty hand and wait for Him to exalt us at the proper time. (See James 4:10 and 1 Peter 5:6.)

2. Answers will vary.

3. Answers will vary.

Thursday—Psalm 4:6–7

1. Answers will vary.

2. Many times, our Lord calms His child before He calms the storm that distresses us by reminding us of His presence, of His Word of promise, of the

mark of ownership He placed on us in Baptism, and, through the forgiveness conveyed to us in the Holy Supper, of the tremendous price Jesus paid for us on Calvary's cross. The "light" of His face evokes imagery of His smile, His favor. He "beams" when He considers us, His redeemed children. The joy of sins forgiven is far more precious than temporary earthly pleasures. In God's favor, we find comfort and take pleasure.

3. Answers will vary.

4. Answers will vary.

Friday—Psalm 4:8

1. Answers will vary. The faith narrative explains the author's choice of this hymn.

2. The Lord gives us sleep as a gift. It refreshes us physically, strengthening us to face our challenges. We can fall asleep in peace, relying on His care for us.

3. Answers will vary.

4. Answers will vary.

Group Bible Study

1. Answers will vary.

2. Listen as group members share.

3. In verses 1 and 3, David recalls the truth that God hears when His children pray. Because of our sin, we have no right to expect our Creator to listen to us, let alone help us. However, He does! And He always will! This is another blessing that flows to us graciously from the mighty cross of our Savior! Share your thoughts with the group.

4. Answers will vary. Note that anger, in and of itself, is not necessarily sinful. The Scriptures describe righteous anger and often attribute it to God. (See, for example, Psalm 18:7 ff.) However, anger can lead us to say and do sinful things. The faith narrative for Wednesday comments in a helpful way about this.

5. David warns us to avoid sinning in our anger; he suggests that we consider our situation in light of God's protecting, sheltering care for us and that we keep on trusting the Lord to bring relief at the proper time. Most important, he urges us to offer "right sacrifices"; when we bring to our Lord

the "broken spirit," the "broken and contrite heart" of true repentance David describes in Psalm 51, we exchange our anger and agitation for the joy of salvation described in Psalm 4:7.

6. Answers will vary.

7. It describes the peace the Lord gives His beloved. The peace that lets us fall asleep in our Savior's arms despite the distress we might still feel comes to us because He is the "God of [our] righteousness" (v. 1), the God who gives us right standing before Him in heaven's court because of what His own Son did for us. Invite other comments, based on the text.

Week 3, Psalm 5

Personal Study Questions

Monday—Psalm 5:1–3

1. The psalmist groans (v. 1) and cries (v. 2) for help. He inserts a lengthy description of the faults of the evildoers (vv. 5–6; 9–10). He pours out a heartfelt complaint to God, asking for vindication and justice.

2. Answers will vary.

Tuesday—Psalm 5:4–6

1. The Holy Spirit has led David to see through His own eyes the pain and destruction evil causes and the insult to God's honor evil imposes. Good and evil are not moral equivalents battling it out on a field of power. Rather, sin has ruined God's original intentions for His creation: that His creatures live in peace, joy, harmony, and love for all eternity. Our pain, caused by evil in the world, breaks God's heart. That's how much He loves us!

While the bullying behavior of others causes us distress, unless we experience pain personally or in our families, we probably do not find the wickedness around us especially distressing or problematic. Most of us must confess that we have grown accustomed, desensitized, to the wickedness of our society. By our own sin and shallow repentance, we have dishonored our Lord. We, too, have acted wickedly, boastfully, and deceitfully. How we need to kneel in true contrition at the foot of Christ's cross, there to receive His gracious pardon!

2. With this understatement, the psalmist calls our attention to God's intense hatred of wickedness and His anger at impenitence and spiritual pride in all its forms. The words "evil may not dwell with [God]" point both the psalmist and us to our desperate need for a Savior. In Jesus, God has removed our wickedness and no longer takes into account the evil we have done. Christ paid our penalty, and, united with Him through faith, we live with God now and forever.

Wednesday—Psalm 5:7–8

1. Verses 4–6 describe the wickedness of the impenitent, those who hate God and rebel against His rule. Verses 7–8 describe those who, although sinners, rely on the Lord's "steadfast love" (v. 7). They "bow" in reverence, acknowledging their need for the salvation their covenant-keeping Savior-God promises to send.

In a sense, the psalmist *is* boasting, but his "boast" is "in the LORD" (see Psalm 34:2). Confident in the Savior's love, paradoxically, the psalmist's attitude is one of God-pleasing humility.

2. Yes, God Himself invites us to come into His presence in confident, expectant hope. We do this, relying fully on Christ's cross, relying on "your [Christ's] righteousness" (v. 8). At the cross, we receive God's full and free forgiveness for our rebellion and wickedness and His unconditional love, love that forever flows to all believers from that cross. God sealed His word of grace to us in our Baptism, and Jesus' righteousness belongs to us, regardless of whether we feel righteous in any given circumstance.

3. Answers will vary.

Thursday—Psalm 5:9–10

1. Like David, we are surrounded by a culture that lies about who God is, what He is like, and what He does for us. Likewise, the world system around us lies about who we are before God.

2. Satan is the "father of lies" (John 8:44). When those who hate God malign Him, disobey Him, or lead others to do so, they are acting as agents of hell. Furthermore, his lies are not benign; they kill—eternally. False teachers are guilty of "soul murder" in that they destroy their followers for all eternity!

3. Sometimes Christians and non-Christians alike associate the

Christian faith with being nice. We need to remember that the same Jesus who taught us to love our enemies threw the money-changers out of the temple, sending their tables and merchandise flying. We do want our enemies to come to repentance and faith, and we earnestly pray for this. How awful it would be if a soul for whom our Lord died would be condemned in hell forever! Even so, we also want God to stop those who pervert the truth and, by their teachings, drag others with them into eternal punishment.

Friday—Psalm 5:11–12

1. Answers will vary.

2. Verse 11 contrasts the rebellion, guilt, and counsels of the wicked with the joy of those who take refuge in the Lord and His righteousness.

3. Answers will vary.

4. Because of what Jesus did for us on His cross, God surrounds us with His favor. He looks on us in compassion and love. He covers us with His grace, a mighty shield of protection against all our enemies—even Satan himself!

Group Bible Study

1. Answers will vary.

2. These verses express the believer's pain in seeing God's Law trampled, God's rule challenged, God's truth denied or twisted, and God's honor besmirched. Answers will vary.

3. The psalmist comes into God's presence, confident of a hearing, confident that the Lord will hear and help. In Psalm 4:1, he appeals to the "God of my righteousness"—to God who makes sinners righteous through faith in the Messiah He covenanted to send. In Psalm 5, the psalmist clings in faith to "my King," "my God" (v. 2). Only by grace can we enter. But knowing God's grace to us in Jesus, we now enter in confident hope and even what some have called "holy boldness."

4. Answers will vary.

5. Aaron's benediction (Numbers 6:22–27) contains similar language. We hear it as each worship service concludes: "The LORD lift up His countenance upon you and give you peace" (Numbers 6:26). The words imply that God welcomes us, considers us His friends, wants only good for us, and will act on our behalf to accomplish that good. Answers will vary.

Week 4, Psalm 6

Personal Study Questions

Monday—Psalm 6:1–3

1. Answers will vary. The psalmist's plea for grace (v. 2) and his description of his troubled soul (v. 3) indicate the depth of his need for forgiveness. Perhaps most telling, however, is his plea that the Lord not rebuke or discipline him as he deserves (v. 1).

2. Answers will vary.

3. Answers will vary.

Tuesday—Psalm 6:4

1. The psalmist appeals only to his need—"I am languishing," "my bones are troubled."

2. He asks that God save him "for the sake of Your steadfast love."

3. Answers will vary.

Wednesday—Psalm 6:5

1. David bolsters his plea that God deliver him by pointing to the fact that "in death there is no remembrance of you." These words are hyperbole, a figure of speech that relies on exaggeration to make an important point. Of course, Scripture elsewhere clearly shows that those in heaven do praise God. See, for example, Revelation 6:9–10. David prefers to praise God here on earth, but his sins have created such a heavy burden that he fears they will crush the life from him!

2. Answers will vary.

3. Answers will vary.

4. See the faith narrative.

Thursday—Psalm 6:6–7

1. Answers will vary.

2. The psalmist describes his tears of grief. He also talks about his deep fatigue, fatigue resulting from sleeplessness; he is crying his way through the

night rather than sleeping.

3. Answers will vary. It would appear, however, that David sees his sins through a more accurate lens than the one we often use today. Our transgressions insult a holy God, a God who has shown only intense love and deep mercy to us. We have been rebellious, unthankful, and self-centered, while our Lord has been good, compassionate, and forgiving. We are truly, in the words of the liturgy, "miserable sinners."

4. Answers will vary.

Friday—Psalm 6:8–10

1. Answers will vary.
2. Answers will vary.
3. Answers will vary.

Group Bible Study

1. Answers will vary. We might pray this psalm in times of personal guilt and repentance; perhaps some participants will mention using the psalm as part of their preparation before Holy Communion.

2. Answers will vary, but participants will likely cite verse 1 as a prayer for mercy and verses 2 and 4 as prayers for grace.

3. Let participants discuss this. Answers will vary. As we tease out the distinction, it may help us remember the seriousness of our sin and the punishment we have earned for ourselves because of it—in other words, our need for mercy. It may also help us remember the incredible lengths to which our God went to secure salvation for us, even sending His own Son to die for us—in other words, our Savior's incredible grace.

4. While David's foes may be other flesh-and-blood human beings, these words more likely refer to sin and Satan, hell and death. By his sin, David has given Satan and his followers more reason to mock God and ridicule His love. (See Romans 2:24 and Psalm 69:6.) In experiencing such deep anguish, David is suffering the pains of hell—albeit in a small way. As he considers the much more extreme punishment of eternal death he has by his sins deserved, it adds to his anguish.

5. Answers will vary.

6. Answers will vary, but should point toward the cross of Jesus and

the freedom He won for us there. Whether we feel like it or not, the truth remains: "The blood of Jesus [God's] Son cleanses us from all sin" (1 John 1:7). God conveys and seals this pardon to us in the Holy Supper and in the absolution spoken by our pastor, week by week. It may be helpful to refer a friend plagued by unremitting guilty feelings to the pastor who has, no doubt, encountered this issue before. However, *all* Christians have the authority from Christ Jesus to assure one another of His forgiveness. (See Matthew 18:15–18 and John 20:23.)

7. Answers will vary. They may include a desire to take one's sins and God's forgiveness each more seriously.

8. Answers will vary. Perhaps your group can use one or more of the prayers as you close today.

Week 5, Psalm 7

Personal Study Questions

Monday—Psalm 7:1–5

1. Answers will vary.

2. Answers will vary. The lament David offers in Psalm 7, seemingly based on accusations of wrongs he did not commit, seems to fit.

3. Answers will vary, but they might include the fact that the words of the prayer remind David of the true rock on which his security rests. He trusts that the Lord will vindicate him, and he waits for that inevitable victory. Similarly, we can trust that our Lord will vindicate us. We need not seek vengeance for ourselves or go on the offensive. In the end—even if it takes until Judgment Day—our innocence will become evident for all to see.

Tuesday—Psalm 7:6–7

1. God's timing is often not ours. Impatient to crawl out from under the pain and strain of problems, we want immediate solutions and deliverance. Often, though, the Lord is working on our behalf in bigger ways than we can imagine. Examples will vary.

2. Answers will vary.

3. Answers will vary.

Wednesday—Psalm 7:8–11

1. Answers will vary.

2. Answers will vary.

3. Answers will vary, but may include the fact that "the LORD judges the peoples" (v. 8)—evil will not continue unchallenged forever. God "test[s] the minds and hearts" (v. 9)—not even secret motives will remain hidden in the Judgment. God is our "shield" (v. 10). He saves the "upright in heart"—those who rely on the right-standing in heaven's court that the Messiah, Jesus, won for us on Calvary's cross.

4. Answers will vary. Every day the wickedness and injustice of our sinful world provoke earth's Judge to indignation. He will bring justice one day, just as He has promised.

Thursday—Psalm 7:12–16

1. The psalm describes ways in which the violence of the wicked falls back on them as a natural consequence. They suffer the violence they themselves planned against others. "Pregnant" with lies and mischief, the wicked find that mischief "return[ing] upon [their] own head[s]" (v. 16). That said, we dare not ignore the fact that God Himself will also "whet His sword" and has "bent and readied His bow" (v. 12) in active preparation for visiting punishment upon the wicked.

2. Answers will vary.

3. The verse begins, "If a man does not repent . . . " and goes on to describe the consequences for impenitent sin. God's gift of repentance (Romans 2:4) represents the doorway through which we escape judgment and to which we invite others. Clinging by faith to Christ's cross, we are saved and safe from the punishment we deserve for the times we have made ourselves guilty of the sins, the deceit, violence, and mischief described in verses 14–16.

4. Answers will vary.

Friday—Psalm 7:17

1. Answers will vary; however, arguably the most important change is that from despair, lament, and anguish as the psalm begins to an attitude of praise and thankfulness as the psalm ends.

2. Throughout the psalm, readers sense the total honesty and transparency before God as the psalmist approaches Him, and the trust on which that

transparency rests.

    3. Answers will vary.

    4. As the psalm begins, David sees the truth about the wicked—their prosperity, impunity, violence, and impenitence. However, he does not see the whole truth—the Lord's eventual judgment on the wicked and the justice that will, at last, prevail. As the psalm ends, the psalmist has come into a deeper reliance on the righteousness that comes to him (and to us) by God's grace and belongs to him (and to us) by faith, the righteousness by which we escape the punishment we justly deserve for our own offenses against a holy God ("my righteousness," v. 8). Absorbing the whole truth and relying on it, we join the psalmist in praising God's goodness and wisdom.

Group Bible Study

    1. Answers will vary.

    2. Answers will vary.

    3. We may explain the depth of David's anguish by considering the context. Already fleeing Jerusalem because of his own son's treason, David encounters Shimei. Although David has never harmed Shimei and has a right, as Israel's king, to expect loyalty and help, Shimei instead offers curses and throws rocks. Tired, beleaguered, and careworn, David deeply feels the injustice of his position. Thus the strong language in the psalm.

    David's allowing Shimei to go unpunished was apparently a political maneuver. David acted the way a humble, forgetful ruler would act, not avenging himself or stroking his own ego. His mercy helped to bring the nation back together, reeling as it was after Absalom's rebellion. In showing restraint, David ensured the unity of the nation and his ability to govern going forward.

    In a sense, King Solomon was God's answer to David's prayer in Psalm 7. As David passed responsibility for the kingdom to his son Solomon, he urged Solomon to act in wisdom as he considered the enemies of the Davidic dynasty. David was God's appointed ruler. As the passage from Exodus makes clear, earthly rulers serve us as God's representatives. When Shimei cursed David, God considered those curses directed not at David alone, but also at heaven's High King. Such wicked rebellion could not go unpunished. Shimei's "repentance" (2 Samuel 19:19–20) was likely a convenient ruse he fabricated to save his own skin. Shimei thought he had gotten away with it. But in the end, King Solomon—acting as God's tool, God's representative—brought about the justice for which David had prayed (Psalm 7:6, 9, 16).

Applications to our lives today will vary, but may include:

* For God's people, justice delayed is never justice denied; we can wait in hope and peace, knowing God will vindicate His own children, the children He loves and for whom His Son died.

* God's children need not and must not seek revenge. No matter how grave the hurt we have suffered, we leave our case in our Father's hands, trusting Him to right all wrongs. Several stories from this week's faith narratives illustrate this; the story of Milo in Thursday's reading comes especially to mind.

* Our Lord discerns our true thoughts and motives; we cannot fool Him into thinking we have repented when we have not. We turn to Him, asking for His gifts of authentic repentance and the faith that trusts Jesus' sacrifice for our sins.

4. The "lion" does terrible spiritual damage, "tear[ing] my soul apart, rending it in pieces, with none to deliver." As the 1 Peter passage makes clear, Satan himself is the lion who intends to rip up our souls, destroying us for all eternity.

5. Answers will vary.

6. Neither arrogant nor foolish, the psalmist is instead fully confident in the righteousness God gives by grace to all who rely on Him in repentant faith. This is the "imputed righteousness" Jesus earned for us on Calvary's cross and to which God's Old Testament believers looked forward. (See Romans 3:23–26.)

7. Answers will vary, but will likely include the idea that after reviewing all the facts, the Holy Spirit has drawn the psalmist into a deeper confidence in the truths expressed in verse 10. For David, as for us, God is our shield. He has saved, does save, and will save the upright in heart—those who have received the righteousness of Christ through faith. Outward circumstances may not have changed, but God's repentant, faith-filled children are safe in their Father's care.

8. Answers will vary.

Week 6, Psalm 10

Personal Study Questions

Monday—Psalm 10:1

1. Answers will vary. Sometimes Satan and our sinful flesh try to beat down our confidence in God's love, telling us we are the only ones in all of the history of God's people who have experienced the vexation the psalmists express. By this, our enemies would want to dissuade us from bringing our concerns to our heavenly Father. By inspiring and preserving psalms like those we have studied, the Holy Spirit would invite, encourage, and urge us to come to Him in confidence and honesty, expressing our needs and trusting our Lord to hear and help.

2. In essence, the psalmist asks the Lord, "Why are You just standing there? Why don't You *do* something!?" Whether the questions are sinful depends upon the heart of the one praying these words. Coming to God in honest perplexity and authentic anger at injustice signifies the kind of faith and confidence the Lord honors. (See Psalm 62:8.) On the other hand, it is certainly possible to speak words like those of verse 1 in deep rebellion and disrespect.

3. Answers will vary.

Tuesday—Psalm 10:2–7

1. Answers will vary.

2. Answers will vary. Compare Psalms 3, 4, 5, 6, and 7.

3. Sinful humankind changes little—at least, at heart. Enemies of the cross in Western culture today may wear a more sophisticated façade than that described in the psalms we have examined in this study. However, their arrogant rejection of God's rule (v. 3), denial of their need for a Savior (v. 4), and security in their own abilities (v. 6) remain unchanged over centuries.

4. Answers will vary, but in any case, they stir our hearts to worship in view of the blessings that belong to us!

Wednesday—Psalm 10:8–11

1. Answers will vary; a prayer asking for the gift of contrition and true

repentance would certainly be in order, as would thanksgiving for the pardon that flows from Christ's cross to every penitent sinner.

2. In verse 4, the wicked person says, "There is no God." In verse 6, he deceives himself into believing he will never encounter setbacks or adversity. In verse 11, he comforts himself with the lie that God is too busy with other things to care about what happens to the helpless here on earth. Believing they will never be brought to justice, bullies use such tactics to achieve their selfish goals.

The folly of all three lies seems self-evident on their face. Still, the capacity of sinful hearts to ignore or deny the truth is enormous. Several aspects of postmodern thought provide only the most recent examples of intelligent people, reputable scholars, lulling themselves into spiritual stupor through self-deception (e.g., absolute truth does not exist; people can construct the "truths" they wish to believe about God; and everyone's "truth" is equally viable). See also Jeremiah 17:9.

Thursday—Psalm 10:12–15

1. At this point in the prayer, the psalmist begins to express hope in the Lord's power, compassion, wisdom, and help.

2. Answers will vary.

3. God did not "forget the afflicted"—the suffering Servant who bore our sins to Calvary—but raised Him from the dead. Jesus, voluntarily helpless as He assumed our guilt and absorbed our punishment, committed Himself into the Father's care and received the help for which He prayed. Jesus "broke the arms" of Satan, destroying forever the enemy's power to insist on our damnation, by enduring the eternal death we had deserved. As today's faith narrative reminds us, we know that nothing will ever separate us from the love of God. The fleeting problems of life on this sinful planet do not disprove or destroy our Father's love for us in Jesus. Additional answers are possible.

Friday—Psalm 10:16–18

1. Answers will vary.

2. This reminder works compassion in our hearts, even for our enemies. We have the confident assurance of knowing the high value our Savior has placed on us and the incredible inheritance we have received in Him. How very sad is the end of those who continue to deceive themselves and who face

eternity apart from His love! Our challenges here, though often seeming formidable, are in the end only "light, momentary afflictions" that are "preparing for us an eternal weight of glory beyond all comparison." (See 2 Corinthians 4:16–18.)

3. Answers will vary.

Group Bible Study

1. Answers will vary.

2. Answers will vary.

3. Accept answers drawn from the text; wording will vary, depending on the translation participants use.

4. Answers will vary.

5. Answers will vary depending upon the translation participants use. The Lord rescues and comforts His own—always! And He uses our troubles to bring us to the Word and Sacraments, where He is present.

6. Answers will vary.